APPROACHING SIMONE

D1603719

Simone Weil, Marseilles, Winter 1941-1942

APPROACHING SIMONE

SIMONE,

A play by
MEGAN TERRY

introduction by phyllis jane wagner

THE FEMINIST PRESS

1973

Published in the United States by The Feminist Press, Box 334,
Old Westbury, New York, 11568.

Library of Congress Cataloging in Publication Data
Terry, Megan.
   Approaching Simone; a play.
   (Feminist Press biography series)
   Bibliography: p.
   1. Weil Simone, 1909-1943—Drama.   I. Title.
PS3570.E7A8   812'.5'4   73-7743
ISBN 0-912670-11-8

Manufactured in the United States of America. Composed by The
Quick Brown Foxes, Bellmore, New York, and by OBU, New
York, New York. Printed by Faculty Press, Brooklyn, New York.

First Edition

CONTENTS

I want to thank Boston University for supporting me during the writing of the first draft of *Approaching Simone* and for producing it so handsomely in connection with their Centennial, and Ellen Stewart for bringing it to New York for five performances at La Mama, and the National Endowment for the Arts for supporting me during the time it took to prepare the final draft for publication by The Feminist Press.

—Megan Terry

APPROACHING
SIMONE

introduction by
phyllis jane wagner

"I accept the universe," a character in one of Megan Terry's plays exclaims; "I accept, not as a furry animal plaything, but as a mind, as a living loving blinding mind."[1]

This is a stunning declaration of human independence. But the speaker's name is Margaret Fuller,[2] and what is most provocative about her declaration is the very fact that she is a girl, a young woman, a female human being: women have publicly declared their human identity in terms of their intellect less frequently in literature than they have in life.

Simone Weil was such a woman and such a mind. Born female, French, and Jewish, she allowed none of these labels—or the stereotyped expectations associated with them—to predetermine the set of her mind or her soul. Her intense desire was to be an active and responsible citizen of Western culture, a culture whose roots lay in Greek civilization and the values of human equilibrium, of a vital, serious, and responsible mind, of truth, of good, of freedom. Weil's love of freedom and

9

her sense of responsibility, combined with her determination to grow beyond the limits society imposed on her because she was a woman, made her uniquely, acutely, and candidly aware of her own limitations. This honesty, toward herself and toward the world, pervades her writing, whether philosophical, historical, political, or personal.[3]

It is the life behind these writings that Megan Terry has dramatized in *Approaching Simone*, highlighting the development and struggles of Simone Weil's mind and spirit from the time she was five years old until her death, in 1943, at the age of thirty-four. In the play, the character Simone exemplifies the gradual liberation of a woman as she transforms herself into a creative person by the concerted efforts of her own will. She is not only the first totally self-aware protagonist to appear in any of Terry's plays,[4] but the first heroic figure as well, and Terry has said that, although she had known about Weil for almost as long as she had been writing plays, it took fifteen years for her to develop the form to contain and the technique to express the breadth and humanity of this modern hero:

I saw a tiny picture of her, and one paragraph about her—it was *seventeen* years ago [i.e., 1955]—in *Time* magazine. It was one paragraph, and it gave two sentences that she'd said. I said, "Why don't I know about this person?" I have been consciously building my technique so that I could write a play about her.[5]

The result of this conscious development of technique is a play unique in Terry's *oeuvre* and rare in the history of dramatic literature—and the playwright is joyfully, rightfully, proud of her achievement:

No one's ever written a play about a genius that worked before. This is the first play at which people kept saying over and over again, "I really believe she was a genius. I believe it!" Which was thrilling to me, that that happened, that that came through. Because many people have tried to write about artists or thinkers, but . . . [6]

Reviewers of *Approaching Simone* (all but one of whom were men, a fact that suggests the extant sex bias in American theatre) unanimously applauded Terry's achievement. Jack Kroll wrote in *Newsweek*:

Miss Terry's play is a chronicle—grave, didactic, warm, filled with an incandescent *interest* in its subject. It is a rare theatrical event for these hysterical and clownish times, a truly serious play, filled with the light, shadow and weight of human life, and the exultant agonies of the ceaseless attempt to create one's humanity.

. . . In her [Simone Weil's] defining of the "longing for an absolute good" as the factor which binds all human beings together, she provides perhaps the only true basis for the creation of new personal and social energies which alone can save men and their society.[7]

To "save men and their society" was indeed one of Terry's hopes in writing *Approaching Simone*—to save human beings and their society. However, the fact that Simone Weil was a female human being is important. It was an important fact of life to Weil, who had to struggle against the oppression she suffered because of it, and important to Megan Terry whose struggles were similar and whose consciousness of insidious sexism, and her attempts to dispel it, have informed the themes of her plays since 1956.

Terry does mean her character Simone to be a model of spiritual strength for all people, but particularly for women; she considers Simone Weil the "balance of Christ—she's the female counterpart, and people have got to have that. Because," she postulates, "we've been living in a homosexual society":

> Men run everything. Male law. Male religion. Women and children have no rights or status, they're only reflections or extensions. We don't live in a heterosexual society at all. That's bullshit. The men look to each other. It's a homosexual society, and we're all suffering from it. We've got to make a balance—a whole half of the human race is not represented, up there, out there, where people can take sustenance from it. There are only male models, and it's too narrow a world to live in. Far too narrow.[8]

It is this narrowness, Terry feels, that has prevented women from creating an identity for themselves, both as women and as human beings:

Women haven't had the time or the opportunity or just haven't taken the power in their own hands to create a model outside of themselves of what's in here, of what they really know. They've imitated masculine models. And when I *saw* this through Simone, I began to get a picture of the possibilities of how to construct—out there for people to walk into—what's going on in here, or what was going on in Simone. *Then* people will say, "My God, it *is* possible; women *are* free to do this and *can*." And once several women have built a few structures, they're going to be building structures all over the place. Because all you have to do is show that it's possible, and then all kinds of people will start adding onto it.[9]

Believing this, and having created her own freedom and identity, Terry feels a personal responsiblity to share it,

to come out and be as strong as I can be for *other women*. They need models, they need to know that a woman can make it and think clearly in a womanly way. All the heroes are dead or killed or compromised, and women *need* heroes. That's why I wrote *Approaching Simone*. . . . I expect that it will affect the world because of Simone's spirit—her spirit comes through. It's a vehicle for her spirit to get in touch with people. Then, I hope, it will direct them to her writing.[10]

In her writings and in this play, Simone Weil stands as a model and incentive for all women to research and contemplate, to evaluate and fulfill their own unique capacities. By the example of their persistent and successful struggles to realize their own self worth, both Simone Weil and Megan Terry offer strength to other women. Because *Approaching Simone* is a play, however, the clarity and dimension of the challenge of these examples rests on the actors' ability to portray them. *Approaching Simone* thus offers a special challenge to the actor. In the history of dramatic literature—from Clytemnestra and Medea, through Lady Macbeth and Cleopatra, to Miss Julie and Blanche Dubois—leading roles for women have usually been found in plays (written by men) in which the basic conflict is sexual: that is, in which the woman's identity is defined in relationship to the man she opposes.

In *Approaching Simone*, the central conflict is internal: Simone is of value in her own right and on her own terms (as Hamlet and Macbeth are). She is a great enough self to confront herself and to be of compelling interest when she does so. She is a great enough soul to be constantly growing from these self-confrontations. She is a strong enough mind to persevere in her desire for intellectual and spiritual truth. And she reaches her goals without compromise. To play Simone is thus a privilege and challenge for any woman. All roles except hers are played by ever-transforming members of the ensemble; she alone remains intransigently herself throughout and thus, as supporting characters change with the changing circumstances of her life, audience attention is focused on Simone from the beginning of the play to the end.[11]

Few scenes in *Approaching Simone* are titled, but one of the most compelling for an audience, and most exciting for an actor, is called "Simone at Fourteen— When and Why She Wants to Kill Herself." She is alone, and members of the ensemble become "aspects of her self-doubt, self-loathing, pain and doubt to torture her." It is a scene symbolic of her entire adolescence. Simone's fears tell her that she has no talent, that she is stupid and awkward, that her mind is as slow as her "miserable body": that she is "nothing but a girl," and will "never amount to anything," will never be as good as her brother—the pain she suffers is proof, it must be some kind of punishment. She will "never know the truth," her mind is too dim. The taunts continue to build, interspersed with suggestions of suicide. Simone, finally concedes: "If I can't find the way to justice and truth, then I don't want to live! I'm mediocre! Only the truly great can enter that transcendent kingdom where truth lives." "Kill yourself, Simone," is the final taunt. But another voice is heard, a voice singing,

ANYONE CAN KNOW TRUTH
DESIRE, DESIRE
ONLY MAKE THE EFFORT OF ATTENTION
FOCUS ON THE DARK INSIDE YOUR HEAD
UNTIL IT LIGHTS YOUR WAY
THE SIMPLEST MAN MAY KNOW TRUTH
IF HE REACHES OUT EVERY DAY.

The calm voice of faith and reason is also Simone's, and it draws her "back to the will to live. From this moment

15

on, she teaches herself, through an effort of pure will, "the art of perpetual attention."

Simone's agony in this scene is total: physical (she suffers from a migraine headache), psychological (she is "only a girl"), intellectual (she "lacks brains"), and spiritual (she desires "truth"). With the use of the transformation technique and an ensemble of actors, Terry is able to capture and demonstrate—theatricalize —every aspect of this unendurable crisis, and the chaos created by the ensemble gives the simple clarity of the Singer's voice and lyrics an appeal that makes their effect on Simone credible.

Analogous to this early scene of tortured self-doubt, is the Visitation scene in Act II. Because physical pain has totally incapacitated her, Simone is unable to work and is therefore on the verge of hysteria:

My spirit is sick. Do I have a spirit. Pains in the throat, double pains. I can't swallow but I feel constantly that I'll vomit. My spine. My spine is sick. I can't work and that makes me sicker. Not to be able to work. No work. Work beating in my head, but my hands refuse to close around a pencil, my mind won't work for me but something in me is working, and I'm so sick and weak. The struggle against this stupid body is getting too much to bear. I've got to think my way out of it but I can't think. My God, my God, I can't think. I can't move, out of this bed, my God I can't stand. I can't walk. I can't think, I can't think, this stupid pain. My God. My God, I need something. I need something. I need my work. I need to work. Any work. I'd cry for joy to be able to bend in the dirt and pick up potatoes till my back ached from work. Honest work, not the work of fighting this endless headache. I'll try to vomit. I'll get it out, I'll vomit out the illness. Oh my God, can't I get any light into my head? My God! My God! My God!

Although her heritage was Jewish, religion had been no more than a matter of abstract speculation for Simone until now. Her use of the name of God here is expletive rather than incantatory. Something strange and marvelous comes of it, however:

The ENTIRE CAST comes on stage and lifts SIMONE up, giving her a total caress. They hum. They take away her pain into their bodies until all but five who lift her up to God are feeling the pain that Simone had. As they lift SIMONE, they take her clothes off, and as the clothes fall, other actors put them on, continuing a pain center at a point in the body the garment covers. They lift her straight up if they can, her arms outstretched, smiling with her eyes closed.
They put her down and exit.

Simone is now "transfixed with divine love," and in this state she sings George Herbert's poem, "Love." In her *Notebooks*, Simone Weil wrote: "Examples of perfect poems, i.e., having a beginning and end, and a

17

duration which is an image of eternity. There are few of them. . . . 'Love' of Herbert is one."[1][2] Appropriately, Terry associates a love poem that Weil considered perfect with Simone's mystical experience of God's love, and the association leads, quite credibly, into a musical rendering of Simone Weil's explanation of why God created human life.

This is the beginning of Simone's mystical vision of human life and of her carefully constructed arguments for the value of human suffering. Near the end of the play, she is delivering a public lecture to members of the ensemble who gradually leave the stage and take up sides to fight the war. Simone is analyzing the stupidity of France's involvement, of its continuing involvement, in World War II. As she speaks, lights begin to flicker and go out. *"PEOPLE crawl on aisles and over audience. Lights—flashing: crying, running."* Her point is that once a war begins, its original objective is lost and the war is perpetuated only as "its importance is imagined as corresponding to the deaths incurred and the further massacres expected." Silence. The war in the theatre begins again, and Simone analyzes war in terms of the relationship between politics and language:

For our contemporaries the role of Helen is played by words with capital letters. If we grasp one of these words, all swollen with blood tears, and squeeze it, we find it is empty. . . . Words without content and meaning are not murderous. When empty words are given capital letters, then men on the slightest pretext will begin shedding blood. In

18

these conditions the only definition of success is to crush the rival group of men who have a hostile word on their banners. When a word is properly defined, it loses its capital letter and can no longer serve either as a banner or as a hostile slogan.

Screams. Someone is shot while pleading not to be. Silence.

It becomes simply a sign, helping us to grasp some concrete reality, concrete objective or method of activity. To clarify thought, to discredit the intrinsically meaningless words and to define the use of others by precise analysis—to do this, strange though it may appear, might be a way of saving human lives.[13]

Someone accuses Simone of being typically "like a woman to reduce war to semantics." A woman retorts, "how like a man to reduce war to mathematics."

The war in the theatre is over, and for the play's penultimate scene the women drag the bodies of the men to "a pile on stage." Simone addresses the wounded veterans in their hospital beds with words intended to comfort and enlighten. Because they are in a constant state of affliction, she tells them, they are more aware of life, their consciousness of life is more acute "than those dying in the war... because they are taken unaware." Speaking from her own experiences with pain, she assures them that their suffering has made them "ready to think." That is, they have only the thinnest shell to break before merging from the darkness inside the egg into the light of truth. It is a very ancient image. The egg is the world you see. The bird in it is Love, the Love which is God Himself and which lives in the depths of every man, though at first as an invisible seed.

She is trying to awaken them to Grace, to the necessity of self-transcendence; for when it is achieved "the spirit throws the miserable body in some corner and is transported to a point outside space. Space has become an infinity. The moment stands still." Simone insists on this as she herself is overcome with migraine pain. She conquers it, however, through an extreme act of faith and will, and as the women repeat the phrase "the moment stands still," "singing, facing the audience from stage or in position in aisles," Simone sings and speaks her mystic vision of the value of suffering:

SIMONE (*singing*)
    YOU, WHEN YOU'VE EMERGED FROM
      YOUR SHELL
    WILL KNOW THE REALITY OF WAR
    THE MOST PRECIOUS REALITY TO KNOW
    IS THAT, WAR IS UNREALITY ITSELF.[14]

Speaking: You are infinitely privileged. War has permanently lodged in your body.

WOMEN (*singing*)
    WAR IS AFFLICTION, FORTUNATE ARE
    YOU TO KNOW.

SIMONE War is affliction. It isn't easy to direct one's thoughts toward affliction voluntarily. To think affliction, it's necessary to bear it in one's flesh, driven very far in like a nail,[15] and for a long time, so that thought may have to grow strong enough to regard it.

You have the opportunity and the function of knowing the truth of the world's affliction. Contemplate its reality!

Once again, the substance of Weil's ideas is not immediately graspable by the intellect; but neither is mystical experience itself. What does emerge from this scene is the fact that Simone has finally succeeded in transcending herself. As her song ends, all the men rise and join the women downstage.

As Simone climbs higher upstage it becomes apparent that she herself is hospitalized. Reminiscent of her childhood sacrifices, Simone refuses to eat and climbs higher and higher. Finally she can hardly stand, and her death is announced:

WOMAN DOCTOR (*at an inquest, British accent*) I tried to persuade Simone to take some food and she said she would try. She did not eat, however, and gave as a reason the thought of her people in France starving.

ENSEMBLE whispers: "Strange suicide" over and over.

21

She died on the twenty-fourth of August and death was due to cardiac failure due to degeneration through starvation.

BARITONE (*singing as a judge*) Simone, aged thirty-four, committed suicide by starvation while the balance of her mind was disturbed.

CHORUS speaks:

WOMEN Strange suicide. Strange suicide.

MEN Refused to eat.

WOMEN Strange suicide. Strange suicide.

MEN Refused to eat.

WOMEN AND MEN (*as lights begin to dim on ENSEMBLE*) She refused. She refused. She refused.

WOMAN ONE She wouldn't eat. She wouldn't eat the bombs of the Germans, she wouldn't eat the furnace of the Nazis. She swallowed the pride of France, but it didn't stick to her ribs.

CHORUS Strange, strange, strange, strange, strange—
Simone wouldn't eat.
Simone wouldn't eat.

WOMAN TWO Her soul was full she didn't have to eat. There's no such thing as personality. There's no such thing as a mind when the body dies. The mind can die before the body dies.

WOMAN THREE She wouldn't eat. She wouldn't eat. She wouldn't eat when others starved. She wouldn't eat while Hitler carved the meat of her countryside.

WOMAN FOUR While everyone else lived on spoiled cabbage leaves and boiled rain water, Simone ate nothing.

Blackout on ENSEMBLE.

WOMAN FIVE How thin she must have been. What a tiny coffin they must have buried her in.

Pin spot on SIMONE, dimming slowly, slowly, slowly, slowly to black.

In production, audiences and critics found this final scene very effective: Kevin Kelly wrote that it had "a purity of intent" that was "startling";[16] Clive Barnes described the light "gradually dying to a cold nothingness of dark" as a "superb theatrical coup."[17] Both saw the same production, but in different places—Kelly in Boston, Barnes in New York.

Terry wrote *Approaching Simone* for presentation at the centennial of Boston University where it premiered on February 26, 1970. Directed by Maxine Klein (who had directed Terry's *Comings and Goings* for the University of Minnesota the previous year) the play was performed by Boston University theatre students. The production played only four nights, through March 1, on a set with a pipe scaffold. At Ellen Stewart's invitation, the show moved to La Mama Experimental Theatre Club in New York on March 3, where its new setting was a series of platforms and ramps. After a total of nine performances, only five which were in New York, *Approaching Simone* won Terry an Obie Award for the Best Play of 1969-70.

All the critics agreed with Jack Kroll that Terry's choice for a hero was admirable:

Simone Weil is not at the moment a fashionable thinker, and an unlikely candidate as a hero for the counter-culture. But Megan Terry's play, *Approaching Simone*, may very well stimulate renewed interest, especially among the young, in one of the most powerful minds and tormented spirits our age has produced. The French Jewess who died in 1943 at the age of 34, was a witness to the dislocations of an age second to none in the intensity of her suffering and her radical effort to see into the depths of the human condition and to find a pattern that would bring meaning and succor to it.[18]

If there is a major problem in *Approaching Simone*, it may be the paradox posed by the "pattern" of Simone's own life, a pattern that was no doubt influenced, despite her attempts to be free, by the traditional role of women, and a paradox created by all mystics who attempt to change the world by withdrawing from it. Early in her life, Simone finds "meaning and succor" in work. As she intimates in her night club speech, work is almost a god to her; it is a "sequence of actions that have no direct connection either with the initial emotion, or the end aimed at"; it is a *Ding an sich* and the only "constant factor" in the world. Thus she dedicates her life to constant work, to constant physical and mental activity, and in her most extreme pain before the Visitation she is tortured most by enforced inactivity, by her inability to work.

And so, following the liberal impulses that move her from the time she is a child, impulses that spring from her concern for individual lives and rights and that find expression in her generosity and willing self-sacrifice, Simone plunges herself into liberal activities and works for liberal causes most of her short life. She does not discriminate in her efforts to help humanity or in her work for a better world; she plunges head on into every new liberal group or movement she finds and, lacking discrimination, she is constantly hurt—by school boards, by workers, by the "Anarchist Forces," by officials in her own French army. Disappointment after disappointment, produced by her abortive efforts to rehabilitate the material world, lead her to a purely spiritual solution to humanity's suffering and to a total break with and denial of the world as it is.

With this turn toward the spiritual, Simone is in one way the obverse of Goethe's Faust. Whereas Faust is finally able to say, "Linger on! You are so fair!" to the moment when he creates an earthly "paradise" by draining swamps and building dikes to create a land in which men will have to reconquer nature's threats every day—that is, in the moment when he creates beneficial and perpetual work and activity for humanity—Simone cries, "Let this moment stand still" when she is able to deny not only human activity and work, but all other aspects of the material world as well. Eventually she withdraws completely.

As one who found strength and wisdom in her thoughts and in the living of her life, I am disappointed. The spiritual solace Simone sought in Divine Love is one alternative to enduring political oppression. This alternative, however, consists of ignoring rather than ameliorating actual human conditions. In her detachment, and because Simone chose to see the human world only in the context of what was already established, she forsook it as well as her own physical life.

And she sacrificed her life in complete passivity, accepting her own pain—and the world's—as necessary preludes to "reality," as preludes to the union with God in spiritual harmony. The necessity of suffering, of being passive in the face of suffering, and of self-sacrifice, are the essence of Christian thought; in traditional sexist thought, they are the essence of womanhood as well, and the two doctrines were at times associated in Weil's mind. In her *Notebooks*, for example, although marriage never preoccupied her, she longed to become "the bride of Christ": this was one of the few times she longed for an identity contingent on someone else—male, god, or otherwise. The dynamics of her life were exciting because, as an individual and as a woman, she was always moved to action and to thought by injustice and a respect for human life. This is why the sacrifice of her own life and thereby her thought seems a capitulation.

But Terry has created a dramatic life which stands in no need for apology: Simone is a model for all people to emulate, a model of intellectual curiosity and integrity in her intense desire and will to continue to search for truth. Before she could begin her search, however, she had to overcome obstacles that men never confront—the cultural obstacles to being a woman. Her life, therefore, is an especially valuable model for other women. "I love him who wants to create beyond himself," Nietzsche wrote, "and thus perishes." Change the pronouns, and therein lies the essence of *Approaching Simone*.

NOTES

1. Megan Terry, *Calm Down Mother* (New York: Samuel French, Inc., 1966), 5-6.

2. Terry named her and modeled her spirit after the nineteenth century American feminist and literary critic.

3. See the bibiliography on page 135 for a complete list of those works of Simone Weil which have been translated into English.

4. See the bibiliography on page 138 for a complete list of Megan Terry's plays.

5. Megan Terry, personal interview, March 4, 1972.

6. *Ibid*.

7. Jack Kroll, ."Waiting for God," *Newsweek* LXXV (March 16, 1970), 64.

8. Terry interview.

9. *Ibid*.

10. *Ibid*.

11. In this respect, the playwright's technique reinforces the play's content; in her persistent and successful self-creation Simone is both rare and fascinating.

12. Simone Weil, *Notebooks* I, trans. Arthur Wills (New York: G.P. Putnam's Sons, 1956), 5.

13. This was one of the implicit premises of *Viet Rock*.

14. Perhaps this is an accurate paraphrase and explication: when individuals break through the shell of their material lives (which encompass corporeal conflicts and sufferings, the highest example of which is war), they realize that life was "unreal"; that is, they realize that the only true reality is spiritual harmony found in the union, through love, with God. They can break through the shell, however, only if they realize it exists. Suffering proves that it exists, and that is why *Simone* tells the veterans they are fortunate.

15. The "nail" conjures the image of the crucifixion, and it is a reminder of Terry's belief that Weil is the female balance of Christ.

16. Kevin Kelly, "B.U. Produces Terry's *Approaching Simone*," Boston *Globe*, February 28, 1970, p. 8.

17. Clive Barnes, "Stage: Terry's Simone," *NYT*, March 9, 1970, p. 43.

18. Kroll, p. 64.

ON
MEGAN TERRY

Megan Terry was born in Seattle, Washington, on July 22, 1932. Originally she planned to spend her life "doing theatre in the Northwest,"[1] supporting herself by teaching creative dramatics in grade school. Her desire to pursue an orthodox teaching career was quelled, however, when she was confronted with a classroom situation while practice-teaching in 1956:

> When I was face to face with the children and listening to what I was saying to them, I realized that I was just a little robot; stuff was coming out of my mouth to train them the way I had been trained. . . . When I realized that, I quit teaching.[2]

When she sensed her growth as a theatre artist was being stunted rather than nurtured at the Cornish School of Allied Arts, she also resigned her directing post there. Although she used pseudonyms and therefore her colleagues did not know she wrote plays, they were "horrified" by the scripts she chose to direct ("by both me and O'Neill"), and Terry refused to give up the right to choose her own material.³ In June she graduated from the University of Washington with a B.A. in Education, and then returned for her fourth and final summer at Banff to receive Certificates in Acting, Directing, and Design.

Her affiliation with educational and theatrical institutions of the Northwest thus terminated, she left Seattle for the East Coast at the age of twenty-four: "I decided New York would be more hospitable to the direction I felt I had to take in my theatre work and it was."⁴

Free of the need to use pseudonyms and more confident of her identity as a playwright, Terry realized that the problem of identity was ultimately a political one. For example, in *Ex-Miss Copper Queen on a Set of Pills* (1956), she investigated the anomolous and therefore destructive nature of pioneer values in an urban habitat, especially the nature of the soul-destroying sexist roles those values impose: a woman's mind and soul disintegrate because she lacks any meaningful personal identity. Thus *Copper Queen* and Terry's other early plays, despite their conventional dramatic forms, clearly reject establishment values; the search for new values is vague, however, and characters (like Copper Queen) who do search are defeated.

By 1960, Terry had sensed that old forms were inadequate to express new ideas, and the pursuit of new values was accompanied by a search for new forms. *The Magic Realists*, for example, a one-act play about the evils, human inadequacies, yet undeniable power of big business and big government, was written in a style Terry refers to as "magic realism."

Working closely with the Open Theatre from 1963-66, her political and aesthetic concerns were shared by other artists, and Terry began to develop uniquely personal styles and forms. Several of the transformation plays she scripted especially for the Open Theatre—*Calm Down Mother*, *Keep Tightly Closed in a Cool Dry Place*, and *The Gloaming, Oh My Darling*—deal with problems of sexual identity, with the pervasiveness of sexist roles in our culture, and with their death-in-life ramifications. Eventually, group work on transformations, a common interest in finding new ways to involve audiences, and a common political concern culminated in the creation of *Viet Rock*, the first American play to deal directly with the Vietnam war, the first rock-musical, and the first play in which actors left the stage to touch members of the audience.

After leaving the Open Theatre, Terry deepened her interests in broad national and political issues, and in plays like *The People vs. Ranchman*, *Home*, *Jack-Jack*, *Massachusetts Trust*, and *The Tommy Allen Show* she concentrated on the chronic ills of social and political identity in America.[5] Her negations of establishment values became clearer as she found new and better ways to express them, but the quest for new values still took the form of questioning, and positive alternatives were only intimated.

In 1969-70, this search culminated in form and content, when Terry transcended national boundaries.

Concentrating on the universal human values often masked by cultural sex roles, she illuminated new roads toward political and personal regeneration in *Approaching Simone*.

At present Megan Terry is at work on her own version of the Don Juan legend. Like *Approaching Simone*, *Don Juan* is an attempt to awaken contemporary consciousnesses to new ways of knowing the world, and in spite of the fact that her most positive protagonist to date (Simone) found strength in celibacy, Terry's belief in the necessity of integrating the respective capacities of mind and body has permeated all of her work. In every play until *Approaching Simone*, it was expressed in terms of the destructive effects of mind dominated by body; *Simone* exemplified body dominated by mind. In contrast to *Approaching Simone*, however, in which Terry affirms one mode of dealing with the world by dramatizing a sexually abstinent life climaxed by an epiphany of divine love, *Don Juan* incorporates an affirmation of the obverse. Here Terry is exploring human love and the epiphanies which can be known only through the act of sexual communion:

> It's very hard to talk about, because it's just opening up in my head—the vast area of human knowledge and human insight that comes from love-making, aside from emotional fulfillment and orgasm. In the process of making love, there is so much creativity. In *Don Juan* I dramatize the insights you get from making love. The act of love is just the entrance to the path of a certain kind of knowledge. I think it's something many, many

33

people know, but they never bring it into the open to examine it.

I hope it isn't peculiar only to me, this kind of knowledge, . . . it's probably a very common thing, but it just hasn't been articulated and set forth. There's a spiritual path to redemption in love-making; there's a whole positive side of love-making that has never, ever, ever been written about. They way our transformations are developing, with this vocabulary of transformations, I think I'll *find* a way of dramatizing it so that it will be available to other people.[6]

Work on an imminent production of *Don Juan* was halted because in Terry's play Don Juan is a woman, and her co-producer (male) decided the play was "too harshly female":

He wants to now work on the Faust legend. But we're beyond that and it doesn't matter; man has symbolized his brain as God and his gentials as the Devil—it's as sinful and infantile as that. We've got to get beyond that now, and inhabit our total bodies and have a marriage of the genitals and the brain. And let's go forward.[7]

Let's go forward to become total human beings.

NOTES

1. Megan Terry, telephone conversation with the writer, May 12, 1972.

2. Megan Terry, personal interview, March 13, 1972.

3. Megan Terry, personal correspondence with the writer, June 2, 1972.

4. Megan Terry, personal correspondence with the writer, April 26, 1972.

5. Plays like *Ranchman* and *Viet Rock* were at first received overseas (particularly in Scandanavian countries) more openly and with more interest and acclaim, than they were in the United States of America.

6. Megan Terry, personal interview, March 4, 1972.

7. *Ibid.*

Please go directly to the writings of Simone Weil. She can transport you to "the tree of illuminated life."

—Megan Terry

APPROACHING
SIMONE

Characters

Simone
Father
Mother
Brother
Visitor
Simone (a college friend of Simone's)
Albert
Jean-Paul
Carolina
Board Head I
Board Head II
Several French military men (all played by the same actor)
The Ensemble
Queens
Kings

ACT I

The stage of the proscenium opening should be raked
at a high enough angle so that any floor movement or
choreography can be seen from anywhere in the house.
Throughout the auditorium should be built at least five
small platforms, covering the theater seats, with stairs or
ropes or bridges for the actors to reach them. There
should be a balcony to stage left and stage right where
the opera singers will stand and sing in spotlights when
necessary. Coming out from the proscenium opening
on both stage right and stage left should be two platforms against the house walls, wide enough to hold
ornate chairs and from four to eight actors each. On
stage right platform, which should be lower than the
height of the main stage but high enough that the
audience can see heads and shoulders, should be male
actors, dressed in the costumes of kings, emperors,
presidents, prelates, etc. They are all very very old.
On stage left platform jutting out from the proscenium
are female actors dressed in haute couture of the thirties.
They are anybody's idea of society and culture leaders.

They are very very old.
Draped above the proscenium opening are the inter-
mingled flags of France, Nazi Germany, Russia, England,
and the United States. In the center of the flags is a
giant ikon, painted in muted, glowing colors and il-
luminated with gold leaf, of God in a flowing white
beard at the top, Jesus below and to the left, a golden
glow below and to the right.
In the corners of the proscenium arch where the arch
and the walls of the house join, stage right and stage
left, are papier-mâché cherubs painted in gold. They
stand from floor to ceiling. In their belly buttons are
golden rings: to the rings are attached golden cords.
The cords are held by the old men and old women
and will be pulled at the appropriate time.
On the ceiling is a beautiful head with an open mouth.
The COMPANY enters from back of the auditorium
in procession. As they reach the stage, they turn and
face the audience. The woman who plays Simone takes
up position at extreme stage left and silently stares at
the audience. The COMPANY sings.

ALL

    THE DARKNESS, THE DARKNESS
    I'M NOT AFRAID OF THE NIGHT
    THE DARKNESS, THE DARKNESS
    WHERE I GROPED INSIDE
    I LOVED THE LIGHT ON THE SNOW
    I SENT MY SUGAR TO THE WAR
    I WATCHED GOOD FRENCHMEN

GO
INTO THE GROUND
BUT I PAID ATTENTION TO THE SOUND
OF THE POUNDING DARK
WITHIN MY HEAD
I FOLLOWED WHERE THE HEARTBEAT LED
AND MY MIND SEEMED TO BLEED

BARITONE

IF THE FOOL PERSISTS IN HIS FOLLY
HE WILL BECOME WISE
IF THE FOOL PERSISTS IN HIS FOLLY
HE WILL BECOME WISE

DESIRE! DESIRE! DESIRE! DESIRE!
ECSTASY! MIND ECSTASY! DESIRE!
DESIRE!
ECLIPSE THE FIRE OF THE SEXUAL DRIVE
REACH OUT THROUGH THE MIND
LEAVE THE SPERM BEHIND
LET THE EGG FALL WHERE SHE MAY
DRIVE, DRIVE, DRIVE
TO MIND ECSTASY

The CHORUS keeps singing "Attention, Attention."

WOMAN

ANYONE CAN BECOME
ANYONE CAN BECOME

MAN

> ANYONE CAN KNOW TRUTH
> ANYONE CAN KNOW TRUTH

ALL

> DESIRE DESIRE!

DUET

> ONLY MAKE THE EFFORT OF ATTENTION
> ONLY MAKE THE EFFORT OF ATTENTION
> STAY IN THE DARK INSIDE YOUR HEAD
> *(Repeat)*
> TILL IT LIGHTS YOUR WAY

ALL

> ATTENTION, PULL WITH YOUR WILL
> GENIUS IS INVISIBLE.

One by one everyone sings the name "Simone" on a different note, then everyone taking her or his same note sings the name "Simone" five times together.

ACTOR *(intones from platform)*   Simone taught herself the art of perpetual attention. Simone taught herself the art of perpetual attention.

Exit.

No matter what age SIMONE is during a scene, she always behaves and speaks as if she were somewhere near thirty.
SIMONE enters running and flings herself down. Her family follows. They mime carrying luggage.

MOTHER   Get up, Simone. We have a long way to walk to the lodge.

SIMONE   I have nothing to carry.

MOTHER   You're too little.

FATHER   You don't have to carry anything.

BROTHER   You can't carry anything, you're only five.

SIMONE   I can carry anything.

MOTHER   Get up at once.

SIMONE   I can carry as much as Brother.

FATHER   My dear little girl. Father can carry you and the luggage too: climb on my back.

SIMONE   I want to carry my share.

MOTHER   There's no need.

BROTHER   You're melting the snow.

MOTHER   You'll catch pneumonia.

FATHER   T. B.

BROTHER   I'm starving. Come on, Simone.

SIMONE   No.

MOTHER   Simone.

SIMONE   No.

FATHER   Simone.

SIMONE   No.

MOTHER   You'll get bronchitis, you'll get the flu,
you'll have a headache, your clothes will be wet. You'll
not sleep a wink. I won't sleep a wink. I'll be up all
night with you coughing. You're too frail, you were not
only ill all this fall, but you were in bed most of the
summer. Please, my little darling, come now and take
Mama's hand.

SIMONE   No. I can carry as much as he can.

BROTHER   Let's see.

SIMONE stands up and BROTHER mimes transference

44

*of luggage on his back to Simone's back. She wobbles,
gets her balance, and slowly trudges ahead.*

MOTHER   What will we do with her, she'll break her
bones before she's six.

FATHER   Let her have her way. She can't keep it up.

BROTHER *(running off)*   ~~I'll eat up all the croissants.~~

MOTHER and FATHER freeze.

*This series of scenes should be played very quickly
in different pools of light.
BROTHER and SIMONE.*

BROTHER   Do you know your Racine?

SIMONE   Of course.

BROTHER   Then whoever dries up first gets slapped
by the other.

He begins to recite Phaedra. *He stumbles. SIMONE
slaps him and continues the passage. She falters and
he slaps her.*

BROTHER   Continue.

SIMONE continues to recite; she gets slapped twice.

Continue. Continue.

VISITOR, MOTHER, BROTHER, SIMONE.

BROTHER   I solved all the math problems before the teacher could.

MOTHER   He's been first in his class in everything since he started school.

VISITOR   He's the genius, and *(pointing to SIMONE)* she's the beauty.

SIMONE turns away as if slapped by an invisible hand.

SIMONE, BROTHER, and MOTHER.

MOTHER   My dearest children, where are your stockings?

BROTHER   We gave them away.

MOTHER   It's raining and freezing out.

SIMONE   The workers' children don't wear stockings, and neither do I!

MOTHER   I won't permit this. Your father won't permit this. You're not to leave the house till I send out for more stockings for you.

SIMONE   I will never wear stockings again.

SIMONE and MOTHER: SIMONE is pouring sugar into an envelope.

MOTHER   My precious baby, my own, my darling, what are you doing with that precious sugar? It was so hard for me to get. I had the maid stand in line for three hours for it.

SIMONE   I'm mailing my sugar to the soldiers at the front.

MOTHER   But why?

SIMONE   They don't have any.

At the beach: FATHER and SIMONE. SIMONE is
gazing at the sunset. (The ENSEMBLE become waves,
gulls, shore birds, etc.)

FATHER   Simone, you've been sitting looking out
over the water for hours—go and play with the other
children.

SIMONE   It's so beautiful. I'd much rather watch the
sunset than play.

She screams a long agonized scream. The ENSEMBLE
rush upstage and turn with their mouths open in mirror
agony.

Father, I have an impossible headache. I've never never
known such pain. It's driving me out of my mind.

FATHER   It's probably only connected to your
menstrual cycle. This often happens the first few times.

SIMONE   It's not like an ordinary pain. I'm going
blind. I'm afraid I'll vomit.

FATHER *(feeling her forehead)*   You don't have a
fever. Where's the pain centered?

SIMONE   It started in my left eye and now has
traveled to the right. I can't stand the light. I can't

48

stand the noise. The noise in the street is trampling
on my brain.

FATHER   Sounds like a migraine. I hope not, my
precious child. Go and lie down in your room. I'll bring
an ice cloth for your head, and make it very dark until
you feel better.

Exit.

a scene symbolic of Simone's adolescence is titled

Simone at Fourteen—When and
Why She Wants to Kill Herself

SIMONE is alone in her room with the wet cloth. *suffering from a migraine with a wet cloth on her head* *As
her pain and anguish build, aspects of her self-doubt,
self-loathing, and pain and anguish appear to torture
her. Each one brings a larger and larger piece of white
wet cloth until she is all wrapped up except for her
head, with a piece left to strangle herself (or one giant
white cloth can be used).*

SIMONE   Oh Father, Father, it's unbearable. Surely
it's some kind of punishment.

ONE   You have no talent, Simone.

TWO   You're stupid, Simone.

THREE   You're awkward, Simone.

FOUR   Not only is your body miserable, but your
mind can't move either.

FIVE   You're nothing but a girl, Simone.

SIX   You'll never amount to anything, Simone.

SEVEN   You'll never match your brother, Simone.

EIGHT   You're only a girl, Simone.

Taunts from the auditorium in three languages,
equivalent to "You're nothing but a stupid cunt."

NINE   The pain in your head is evidence.

TEN   Evidence of your lack of brains, Simone.

ELEVEN   You'll never know the truth, Simone.

TWELVE   Your mind is too dim to perceive the
truth, Simone.

THIRTEEN   Put an end to your stupidity, Simone.

FOURTEEN   Beauty is useless, Simone; it isn't the
path to the truth.

FIFTEEN   You're unworthy, Simone.

SIXTEEN   You're wretched, Simone.

SEVENTEEN   You're unfit for this world, Simone.

EIGHTEEN   You're arrogant, Simone.

NINETEEN   You'll never create anything, Simone.

TWENTY   You have no talent, Simone.

TWENTY-ONE   You have no genius, Simone.

TWENTY-TWO   You're a girl, Simone.

TWENTY-THREE   Your pain is your proof, Simone.

TWENTY-FOUR   You're always sick and you'll always be sick, Simone.

TWENTY-FIVE   Your head will always ache, Simone.

TWENTY-SIX   You can't even draw a straight line, Simone.

TWENTY-SEVEN   You have poor circulation, Simone.

TWENTY-EIGHT   Your hands are always swollen, Simone.

TWENTY-NINE   It takes brains to discover the truth, Simone.

SIMONE   If I can't find the way to justice and truth, then I don't want to live! I'm mediocre! Only the truly great can enter that transcendant kingdom where truth lives.

THIRTY   Kill yourself, Simone.

THIRTY unrolls the white sheet. SIMONE rolls tortuously out. As the SINGER sings, SIMONE is drawn back to the will to live. She slowly rises.

SINGER
>ANYONE CAN KNOW TRUTH
>DESIRE, DESIRE
>ONLY MAKE THE EFFORT OF ATTENTION
>FOCUS ON THE DARK INSIDE YOUR HEAD
>UNTIL IT LIGHTS YOUR WAY
>THE SIMPLEST MAN MAY KNOW TRUTH
>IF HE REACHES OUT EVERY DAY.

A nightclub. SIMONE sits smoking buried behind the menu. Her friends SIMONE, JEAN-PAUL, ALBERT, and some others sit around tables. There is a small band playing in the background.

SIMONE TWO   Simone, roll me a cigarette.

JEAN-PAUL   She's too clumsy.

ALBERT   She's getting better.

SIMONE TWO   They burn longer—she packs them tight.

JEAN-PAUL   Simone, your lips.

SIMONE   Eh?

ALBERT   You're reading the script off the menu.

JEAN-PAUL   She won't order anything anyway.

ALBERT   I'll order for her. Tonight we eat.

JEAN-PAUL   Tonight we drink. Whiskey!

SIMONE TWO   Whiskey! Whiskey, Simone?

SIMONE   No.

SIMONE TWO   Here, take my tobacco.

SIMONE   Thanks.

JEAN-PAUL *(watching SIMONE roll cigarette)*
Hey, she's doing it with one hand.

ALBERT   American.

SIMONE TWO   Twist the end, like yours. Ah.

*SIMONE, rolling cigarettes in each hand, drops them
and gets tobacco all over her skirt, the table. She tries
to brush it together. Everyone sputters.*

JEAN-PAUL   Get it out of the way. Carolina is
almost on.

SIMONE TWO   We were lucky to get in.

ALBERT   I'm in love with her.

SIMONE   How long has she been in France?

ALBERT   I hope she never leaves; she's promised
never to leave.

SIMONE   I'd like to talk with her sometime.

*Her friends laugh. Successfully rolling another cigarette
for herself, she lights it with the stub of the one in her
mouth.*

They've been so exploited. We do the same in our
colonies. How can you sit here drinking and grinning
like apes when we are grinding down the blacks in
Africa?

JEAN-PAUL   We'll change all that tomorrow.
Tonight we have fun.

SIMONE TWO   Simone is right. Have you written a
position paper on the colonies?

JEAN-PAUL   I will, I will. I have to form a coalition
with the workers first.

ALBERT   It won't be hard. The monetary system is

55

cracking. I predict within six months, a year at most, we'll have no trouble recruiting.

JEAN-PAUL   The international capitalistic beast has fed on itself so long, it won't find even a kernel of corn left in its shit to keep it going.

SIMONE   It's beginning to happen in Germany. I plan to go there to examine the new workers' alliances at first hand.

JEAN-PAUL   I'll publish anything you send back.

SIMONE   Good. but I won't have much time to write. I intend to work.

ALBERT   Work, work. Always work. Whiskey!

SIMONE   Everything begins and ends with work. Work is constant. You and I pass through, but the work is always here.

SIMONE TWO   One day the machines will do all the work.

SIMONE   If we are not careful, we will work for the machines.

JEAN-PAUL   Technology will free man from manual labor.

SIMONE   I hope not.

ALBERT   What is so sacred about working with your
hands. I've never worked with my hands and I never
intend to—we're freed from that.

SIMONE   You are privileged; they are not.

ALBERT   I want to think; I want to plan, create.

SIMONE   You above all should understand work.
Work, in contrast to reflection, to persuasion or to
magic, is a sequence of actions that have no direct
connection either with the initial emotion, or the
end aimed at . . . Colors, sounds, dimensions can
change, while the law of work, which is to be end-
lessly indifferent to what has preceded and what will
follow, never changes. Qualities, forms, and distances
change, but the law of work remains the constant
factor to which qualities, forms, and distances serve
only as signs. The law of exterior relations defines
space. To *see* space is to grasp that work's raw
material is always passive, always outside one's self. . .

ALBERT   Whiskey.

SIMONE TWO   Here she comes.

JEAN-PAUL   Simone. Attend her closely. Tell me
if Carolina is working or creating magic.

57

SIMONE *(smoking again, she sits back)* Now *you're* working too hard, Jean-Paul.

WAITER Caro—lin—A!!

CAROLINA, a black American entertainer, takes the stage. She sings first in a blues style that changes to a Charleston and then back to a shoutin' blues. She's backed by a mixed chorus who dance in the style of 1928-29.

CAROLINA *(singing and dancing, blues, Charleston, tap, stomp)*
> THE BLUES WAS A PASS TIME
> THE BLUES WAS A PASS TIME
> FOR THAT TIME
> I DIDN'T HAVE NO TIME
> FOR NOTHIN BUT THE BLUES
>
> I COULD SPEND THE DAY
> I COULD LAY THERE ALL THE DAY
> PASSIN TIME WITH MY BLUES
>
> THE BLUES WAS MY PASS TIME
> THAT WAS THE LAST TIME THAT I
> LET THE BLUES GET ME THAT WAY
>
> MY LATEST OLD MAN LEFT ME IN MY BED
> HE WALKED ON DOWN TO THE STORE
> HE'D WATCHED MY RED HEART

TURN TO LEAD
HE SAID "CHILE, CHILE, CHILE,
I JES CAIN'T SLEEP WITH YOU NO MORE."

IT'S PAST TIME FOR THE BLUES
THEY DON'T GONNA GRAB ME NO MORE
I AIN'T LAYIN' WITH THE BLUES
I'M SICK OF THE HEARTSICK
I DONE LICKED THE BLUES

IT'S LONG PAST TIME FOR THE BLUES
MY RED HEART DONE TURNED TO BLUE
BUT ALONG CAME A PRETTY MAN
WHO MADE ME KNOW MY EYES WAS BLACK
HE TOLE ME, BABY, YOU IS MINE NOW AND
YORE OLD MAN AIN'T NEVER COMIN BACK

AND I'M GLAD HE'S GONE
OH YES, I'M GLAD HE'S GONE
I GOT A NEW MAN, NOT A BLUE MAN

HE GIVES ME SUGAR AT NIGHT
HE GIVES ME SUGAR AT NIGHT

HE BAKES MY BREAD
HE HOLDS ME TIGHT

HE CALLS ME HIS PEACHES
I CALLS HIM MY CREAM
HE CREAMS

MY PEACHES
HE CREAMS MY PEACHES,
AND BABY LET ME TELL YOU,
BABY LET ME TELL YOU,
THIS AIN'T NO DREAM!!

They applaud wildly, bang the table; ALBERT jumps up and invites her to the table. She comes over and he introduces her around. She shakes hands. SIMONE crunches down in her chair. She is very shy, lights two cigarettes at once, and starts to pick up the menu again. The band begins a mild Charleston. CAROLINA bends over SIMONE.

CAROLINA   Hello baby, give me some sugar. Hey baby, give me some sugar.

As SIMONE turns red, CAROLINA kisses her on the neck, and then pulls her to her feet.

Come on and Charleston, Charleston with me.

SIMONE   I beg your pardon?

CAROLINA   Dance, baby.

SIMONE   I don't know how.

CAROLINA   Follow me.

SIMONE hands notebook to ALBERT.

SIMONE   I'm afraid I . . .

CAROLINA   Don't work so hard. . . like this, nice
and easy does it. . .

*SIMONE, awkward, makes some attempt. Her friends
are delighted.*

SIMONE   I can't get my hands right.

CAROLINA   You'll get it, you'll get it. Let it come
up through the floor. Let it creep right up ya spine.
Yeah, yeah, you gettin' it. Who's buyin'?

ALBERT *(yelling)*   Whiskey.

JEAN-PAUL   Work or magic, Simone?

SIMONE   It's divine, Jean-Paul.

They all laugh.

ALBERT   So are you. What do you drink, Carolina?

CAROLINA   Old Forrester, neat.

As they exit:

ALBERT   Say you will never leave France. Say you will never leave me.

CAROLINA   Anything you say, baby—it's really true what they said about Paree.

SIMONE remains alone onstage. The ENSEMBLE appears in grotesque gray bags. They move slowly to smother her. She remains in one place.

SIMONE *(a litany)*   What I am, I endure. What I am, I endure. I suffer, I desire, I doubt, I'm stupid. I'm ignorant, I'm not well put together. What I am does not satisfy me. I have become me without my consent. Tomorrow is an I that now I cannot change. What I am, I endure, I suffer.

The ENSEMBLE covers her for an instant. Then break and dissolve upstage. Alone:

I desire, I am stupid! What I am, I endure.

SIMONE and her MOTHER arrive in a truck made of the ENSEMBLE at the rooms where Simone's first teaching post is to be. SIMONE is chainsmoking and reading newspapers and magazines throughout the scene. The truck is loaded with all sorts of furniture,

*etc. The MOTHER directs TWO WORKMEN who
mime unloading and placing the articles. SIMONE
sits, smokes, reads, and makes rapid notes.*

MOTHER   A delightful cottage. Looks tight. I shall
check for drafts. Bring in the furniture.

*SIMONE takes a fast glance and goes back to her reading;
the minute a chair is placed she sits and continues.*

The bed there, the photos there, the commode there,
the bureau there, the table there, the chairs here, the
sofa there, the rug here, no the bed here out of the draft,
now the rug back here, the bureau there, the desk here.

She pays MOVERS. They exit.

Simone, see the view from your desk. You'll be able to
correct your papers while you watch the sun set. Be
sure not to open the window when you work: it gives
you pain in your neck. We'll all miss you and write
every week. Take possession of your pupils; they're
lucky to have you. I've furnished your room. It's
beautiful. See how well everything fits. Be well and
happy and write every week. Do you like what I've
done?

SIMONE *(taking cigarette out of her mouth)*   It's
beautiful, darling.

MOTHER   You must keep well and let me know the minute anything happens. Don't catch cold, and try to remember to eat. Promise me you'll remember to eat.

SIMONE   I promise, my darling mother, and I promise I'll write you both every week.

MOTHER kisses SIMONE, then exits. SIMONE starts to speak but lights another cigarette and methodically rounds up all the furniture except desk, chair, and bed and pushes them over into the orchestra pit. Then she goes to sleep on the floor.

Lights dim a moment—then come up bright morning. Her first class of girls is entering, chattering, and wondering about their new teacher.

ALL   *Bonjour,* etc.

SIMONE rises and waves her hand at them without looking; she's deep in thought.

PUPIL   Does that mean we're supposed to sit down?

They push one another into the classroom, trying to suppress laughter and excitement. The men in the ENSEMBLE have assumed the position of desks— the girls each choose one and sit on his back.

SIMONE *(pacing)*   To teach or not to teach, that is

64

the way to earn my bread. To teach or not to teach. That is the way to earn my soul. I hate to eat. What is feeding?

During all this the GIRLS are secretly looking at her, making fun of her, sizing her up, passing notes and making gestures.

Bonjour mes chers enfants. Bon. It's a good day. Did you see the sunrise?

CLASS giggles.

It's good to get up in time to see the sunrise. You all do it. You have to get to school on time.

CLASS *(bored)* *Bonjour, Mademoiselle.*

They turn off and look out at the audience and stay very stiff while shuffling their feet and picking their ears, or secretly scratching their crotches.

SIMONE   I have some new ideas.

Many groans from CLASS.

They will stimulate your minds.

Many more groans and stamping of feet. SIMONE walks around in agitation. STUDENTS watch her.

Listen to me. If you won't bend a little, I'll have to smoke.

CLASS laughs and claps.

I'm fighting off lighting up a cigarette, because I'm trying to teach you.

CLASS *(sighs, mocking)*   Ohhh!

SIMONE   I've been educated in Paris.

CLASS *(sighs)*   Oooo!

SIMONE   I've been educated by the bourgeoisie to teach you to be like me, and if that is what you want, that is what you'll get.

STUDENT   We knew that before we came. That's why we're here. How else will we get good jobs?

SIMONE   At the same time that I teach you to be like what your parents expect, because I too love and respect my parents and wish to live up to what they respect, I do wish to make some innovations.

CLASS   Not another innovation.

SIMONE   What I as a teacher would like to do with my life is to try to work out with you as I'm working out with myself some of the things important to all of us. Since this class is concerned with the philosophy syllabus, what I'd like to do is to demonstrate to you how philosophy came into being as a name, as a way of thinking; I want you to know the history and the definition of it and not just the name "philosophy" that will be found one day written in your exercise books. I care to speak to you about how to live.

STUDENT *(laughs)*   But we're already alive.

SIMONE   Everywhere?

STUDENT   Where's that.

SIMONE   That is what we'll discover. Class dismissed for today.

GIRLS rise and exit—talking bewilderedly—then return. As they enter the classroom again, they push their desks closer to SIMONE.

SIMONE   *Bonjour.*

CLASS   *Bonjour (Hi—Hello, etc.)*

SIMONE   Who wishes to hike this weekend?

ALL raise hands, with exclamations.

67

We're taking a difficult trail.

Still ALL raise hands, make sounds of assurance.

I think we'll have good weather, and I don't want to miss it before it gets too cold. I want you to begin to take yourselves more seriously as writers. It seems to me a good way to do this would be for you to see your work in print. Therefore, I've procured a printing press, and from now on all compositions in philosophy will be printed. This will mean extra hours because you'll have to learn how to run the printing press, but that will be a good lesson in physics and mathematics as it relates to work.

GIRLS run out while MEN become a printing press. GIRLS slide down a ramp, into the press—MEN stamp them as GIRLS triumphantly laugh and then run out to audience to read to them their bits of poems or philo- sophy. The actors should write or choose these things themselves.* Each GIRL finds several audience members to speak to.
After GIRLS have reached as many audience members as possible, they gather at back of auditorium and begin their hike—over and through the audience.

---

* In the Boston production the actors chose lines from the works of Simone Weil.

SIMONE on a hike with her pupils. They carry packs.
They climb and struggle forward toward the stage.

SIMONE   Let me carry that.

ONE   I can manage.

SIMONE   No, I'll carry your pack. The way is steep.
(To another) Give me yours, too.

TWO   Thank you, *Mademoiselle*. I don't see how
you do it—you don't look that strong. *(To audience
member)* Would you pass my pack across to her?
Thank you.

SIMONE   This is how one becomes strong.

THREE   How does one become in love?

SIMONE   Love?

FOUR   We understand what you teach us about
physics. Could you tell us about love.

SIMONE   Love?

ALL *(on stage now)*   Falling in love. Loving. Being in
love. Is it good or bad?

THREE   I want to know love.

SIMONE   Love?

ALL   Love!

SIMONE   Love is a serious thing.

ALL   Yes. Yes.

SIMONE   I have no advice to give you about love.

ALL   But you must—you know all about calculus.

SIMONE   Love? No, I have no advice to give you but
I must warn you: love is a very serious thing.

ALL *(expectant)*   Yes, *Mademoiselle.*

SIMONE   Love often means pledging one's own life
and that of another human being forever. It always
means that, unless one of the two treats the other as a
plaything. In that case, a love is something odious. The
essential point in love is this: one human being feels a
vital need of another human being. The problem then
arises of reconciling this need with freedom. A problem
men have struggled with from time immemorial.

THREE   But if one is in love and pledged forever,
why would you want to be free?

SIMONE   When I was your age, I was tempted to try

to get to know love. I decided not to. I didn't want to commit my life in a direction impossible to foresee until I was sufficiently mature to know what I wish from life and what I expect from it.

FOUR   But I want to know now.

SIMONE   I'm not offering myself as an example; every life evolves by its own laws. But you might think about it. Love seems to me to involve an even more terrifying risk than blindly pledging one's own existence. I mean the risk, if one is the object of a profound love, of having absolute power over another human being. It's not that one should avoid love, but while you're very young, don't seek it, let it come and find you. Let's say hello to the mountains. There's new snow up there.

They climb higher as SIMONE walks back down mountain to her classroom. She finds several SCHOOL BOARD MEMBERS waiting for her.

HEAD OF BOARD *(holding four other MEMBERS in donkey reins)*   Mademoiselle!

SIMONE walks in front of them reading a newspaper and puffing cigarette smoke like crazy.

SIMONE   M-m-m-m-m-m-m-m. . .

BOARD   *Mademoiselle* Instructor!

SIMONE   M-m-m-m-m-m-m-m-m. . . *(continues to read and smoke).*

BOARD   The board finds that you are not paying attention to the board.

MEN   The board.

SIMONE   M-m-m-m-m-m-m-m-m. . .

BOARD   The board finds that you are not paying attention to the board.

MEN   Attention!

SIMONE   There is not enough time to pay attention the students.

BOARD   You smoke.

MEN   Smoke!

SIMONE   Yes. . . *(starts making note and takes out a cigarette).*

BOARD   You had the effrontery to print the students' work.

MEN   Work?

SIMONE   M-m-m-m-m-m-m-m. . . ?

BOARD   This is nothing but the work of students.

They shake printed papers in front of her.

MEN   Students!

SIMONE   It is the printed word.

BOARD   You were not authorized to print the work
of nobodys.

MEN   Nobodys!

SIMONE   That is how they become somebodys.

BOARD   You are fired.

SIMONE   That is a fact I accepted in advance.

*The SCHOOL BOARD exits in a chaos of entangled
reins. Blackout.*

SIMONE at a new school. It is a tougher school than before—the GIRLS pretend to be blasé—no desks. They enter and stand around in what they think are tough, sophisticated poses.

SIMONE   *Bonjour, Mesdemoiselles.*

CLASS   We don't want *Bonjour.* We want life.

SIMONE   First you must learn to think.

CLASS   We want to live.

SIMONE   What is living?

CLASS   Enjoyment of the now.

SIMONE   If you cannot think, you will be robbed of the riches of the past and the future. To live in the now is pleasurable, but to think in the past and future is necessary to the development of your person and your family; therefore your roots and your country.

CLASS   Teach us to think.

SIMONE   It is hard, but if you pay attention, hard things can bring you good. Who would like to hike with me this weekend?

Some hands up.

74

I have reports that there will be a break up of the ice, and possibly a flood. Who is strong enough to swim through the ice floes?

Rest of hands up.

Bon, meet me at the river bank at three in the morning, with a little food for the two days, and matches wrapped carefully so that we can dry outselves out, if we have to swim or rescue anyone. How many again wish to go on the hike?

All hands up.

Bon. Girls are getting stronger. It's important. It's only through hard work that one understands one's intelligence.

GIRL *(delayed reaction)*   Yeah.

After much reluctance and teasing, they pull off their clothes and one by one dive into an ice river. One GIRL almost doesn't make it, but she's saved by another. They swim to high ground and put their clothes back on again. SIMONE dresses and walks back to the classroom area.

SIMONE walking and smoking in front of the SCHOOL BOARD.

BOARD   *Mademoiselle!*

SIMONE   M-m-m-m-m-m-m-m. . .

BOARD   *Mademoiselle,* You took the students on an unauthorized hike.

SIMONE   A swim. . .

BOARD   On an unauthorized swim under the most dangerous of conditions in the middle of winter.

SIMONE   The sun was out.

BOARD   There had been no permission granted by the school board or by the parents, and in fact you are to be considered under arrest for kidnapping.

SIMONE *(reading and walking and smoking)*
M-m-m-m-m-m-m. . .

BOARD   Three people caught pneumonia.

SIMONE   Five were saved from drowning.

BOARD   Your students saved by other students.

SIMONE   An excellent experience in learning.

BOARD   You have been noticed to smoke and read and not pay attention at teachers' meetings.

SIMONE   M-m-m-m-m-m-m-m. . .

BOARD   You are hereby fired for insubordination, and endangering the lives and the moral attitudes of your pupils. You are hereby separated from us, uh fired, uh terminated.

SIMONE *(walking and smoking)*   M-m-m-m-m-m-m-m. . . It is the condition of my teaching.

BOARD MEMBER *(on way out)*   And remove your coffee cup from the teachers' room.

Exit.

SIMONE meets with her old teacher and master ALAIN.

ALAIN   I've been following your articles closely.

SIMONE   They're only beginnings—I'm so awkward and confused.

ALAIN   No, I've never had a pupil like you. Your power of thought is rare.

SIMONE   All I have so far are hazy outlines and over-weening ambitions.

ALAIN   Simone, on the contrary, it's like a game for you. I want to see you turn from playing games with abstract subtleties and train yourself in direct analysis.

SIMONE   I intend to. I'm going into the fields, I'm going into the factories, I'm going to study the relationship of the worker to his work. Modern science has lost its soul because it reasons only about conventional symbols—objects, they become objects by the fact that they are black marks on white paper, but which are universal by virtue of their definition. There should be a new way of conceiving mathematics—a way that its theoretical and practical value would no longer be distinct, but would reside in analogies. In man's struggle with the universe, symbols would thus be relegated back to their rank as mere instruments, and their real function would be revealed, which is not to assist the understanding but the imagination. Scientific work would thus be seen to be in fact artistic work—namely, the training of the imagination. It would be necessary to foster and develop to the maximum the faculty of conceiving analogies without making use of algebraic symbols.

ALAIN   It sounds like an excellent project, but please, Simone, when you write about it, try to make your language more penetrable to the ordinary mind.

SIMONE   I hope you'll excuse the confusion and disorder and also the audacity of my embryo ideas. If there is any value in them, it's clear that they could only be developed in silence. *(Hurriedly)* Also, I want to do a series of studies of the various existing forms of property, related to the idea that property consists, in reality, of the power to dispose of goods.

Fade on ALAIN as SIMONE walks into her room.

1934. Several ex-pupils come to visit SIMONE in the factory town where she works.

SIMONE   How good to see you again.

ONE   You didn't answer our letters.

TWO   We were worried.

THREE   Have you been ill?

SIMONE   Work in a factory isn't conducive to letter writing. How did you know where I was?

FOUR   The Derieu sisters.

SIMONE   Please don't tell anyone else. Promise me. This is the "contact with real life" we often talked about together.

ONE   But you're so frail.

SIMONE   Clumsy too, and slow, and not very robust.

TWO   How did they hire you?

ONE   There's no work these days.

SIMONE   One of my best friends knows the managing director of the company.

THREE   What's it like?

SIMONE   I'm glad to be working in a factory, but I'm equally glad not to be compulsorily committed to it. It's simply a year's leave for "private study."

As the speech continues, the ENSEMBLE enters and builds and becomes the factory and machines. SIMONE works at her machine, and the speed of her speech builds with the speed of her work.

If a man is very skilled, very intelligent, and very tough, there is just a chance, in the present conditions of French industry, for him to attain a factory job,

Her visitors become machine parts.

which offers interesting and humanly satisfying work; even so, these opportunities are becoming fewer every day, thanks to technical progress. But the women! The women are restricted to purely mechanical labor— Nothing is required of them but speed. . .

The machines begin to work in earnest.

When I say mechanical labor, don't imagine that it allows for daydreaming, much less reflection or thought. No. No. The tragedy is that, although the work is too mechanical to engage the mind, it prevents one from thinking of anything else. If you think, you work more slowly:

The machines slow down and are silent.

BARITONE *(sings)*
    SPEED, SPEED, SPEED
    SPEED, SPEED, SPEED
    SPEED, OR THE SACK
    SPEED, DON'T TALK BACK
    SPEED, SPEED, SPEED
    IF YOU WISH TO FEED.
(Speaks) Hurry up, Simone, you made only six hundred yesterday. If you make eight hundred today, maybe I won't fire you.

The machines abruptly speed again.

SIMONE   I still can't achieve the required speeds. I'm not familiar with the work, I'm innately awkward. I'm naturally slow moving, my head aches, and then I have a peculiar inveterate habit of thinking, which I can't shake off. Believe me, they would throw me out if I wasn't protected by influence. Theoretically, with the eight-hour day, one should have leisure, but really one's leisure hours are swallowed up by a fatigue which often amounts to a dazed stupor. Also, life in the factory involves a perpetual humiliating subordination, forever at the orders of foremen.

THREE   How can you stand the suffering?

SIMONE   I do suffer from it, but I'm more glad than I can say to be where I am. I've wanted it for I-don't-know-how-many years.

The ENSEMBLE slowly breaks up the giant machine and exits, but SIMONE continues to work as she speaks.

But I'm not sorry I didn't do it sooner, because it's only at my age now that I can extract all the profit there is in the experience. Above all, I feel I've escaped from a world of abstractions, to find myself among real men— some good and some bad, but with *real* goodness or badness. Goodness especially, when it exists in a factory, is something real. The least act of kindness, from a mere smile to some little service, calls for victory over fatigue and the obsession with pay—all the overwhelming influences which drive a man in on himself. Thought then calls for an almost miraculous effort of rising above

82

the conditions of one's life. Because it's not like at a
university, where one is paid to think, or pretend to
think. In a factory one is paid not to think. So, if you
ever recognize a gleam of intelligence, you can be sure
it is genuine. Besides, I really find the machines themselves highly attractive and interesting.

*As members of ENSEMBLE arrive very slowly with real
machines which they carry or manipulate, SIMONE
exits, as if in a trance. The ENSEMBLE members stare
and work their machines as if the machines were con-
trolling them. Slow fade.*
*The OLD LADIES pull the cord attached to one cherub.
The belly opens and jewels made of jello and candy
tumble out, showering the audience.*

ACT II

SIMONE enters with materials for letter. As she speaks the ENSEMBLE work out math forms (i.e. equations or symbols) with their bodies.

SIMONE   I need a physicist. I really need a physicist. Dearest Brother, please ask a physicist in America the following question: Planck justifies the introduction of quanta of energy by the assimilation of entropy to a probability (strictly, the logarithm of a probability): because, in order to calculate the probability of a macroscopic state of a system, it is necessary to postulate a finite number of corresponding microscopic states (discrete states). So the justification is that the calculus of probabilities is numerical. But why was it not possible to use a continuous calculus of probabilities, with generalized number instead of discrete numbers (considering that there are games of chance in which probability is continuous)? There would then have been no need of quanta. Why couldn't this have been tried? Planck says nothing about it. T. does not know of any physicist here who could enlighten me. What do you think about this?

The ENSEMBLE recites theories, goes into the audience to lecture them. Each actor should make up his own, outrageous theories or speculations.
The ENSEMBLE says to each other and the audience: "What do you think about this?" as they exit.

SIMONE   Your reply about Planck did not satisfy me. Have you read St. John of the Cross?

Blackout. ENSEMBLE stays in auditorium aisles walking back and forth resolutely with eyes closed whispering: "You don't interest me."

SOPRANO   You don't interest me.

BARITONE   You don't interest me.

SOPRANO   I can't see you.

BARITONE   You can't see me.

SOPRANO   I look right through you. I look right through you because when I look, there is nothing there to see.

BARITONE   You don't interest me.
You don't interest me.

85

A Pharisee interests me more than how
Definitely
You don't interest me.

*SIMONE on stage. This is her inside now: it slowly
comes out as the SINGERS sing, she passes people;
as she passes them, she "fixes" on them. They feel
it, and begin to reach out to her as if in a trance. They
stop short of touching, but their eyes stay locked.*

CHORUS
      YOU HAVE NOTHING FOR ME.
      I WALK RIGHT THROUGH YOU
      YOU DON'T EVEN BORE ME
      I'VE NEVER HEARD YOU

SIMONE *(into mike)*   No one cay say you don't
interest me, without showing grave cruelty and
profound injustice to the uniqueness of the individual
soul.

*The ENSEMBLE actors move up onto the stage and
form moving human structures two and three people
high.*

SIMONE   There is something sacred in every person.

CHORUS   There is something sacred in every person.

SIMONE   But it is not his person.

CHORUS   But it is not his person. Not his person?
Not his person? But if not his person, then what is
sacred in every person, if it is not his person?

SIMONE   It isn't his personality.

CHORUS   How can we sell him.

SIMONE   It isn't his personality, the personality he
carries in his person.

CHORUS   But that's the package.

SIMONE   So much baggage.

CHORUS   Give me a good personality any day, and I
can come with him in every way.

SIMONE   So much baggage.

SOPRANO   I agree with the chorus.

SIMONE   So much baggage.

BARITONE   I wouldn't mind for a while to carry the
chorus for an extra mile.

SIMONE   Not his person, nor his thoughts
that I don't know.
Not his person, nor the way his arms grow.

Not his person, nor the way his eye is lit.
Not his person, but his total sacredness of it.
His presence. His presence that hurts us
when we must do without it.

CHORUS   His presence when we must do without it.
King, Queen, father, father, mother, mother, sister,
brother, friend, friend, friend, when you are gone and
we have to live without your other.

SIMONE   Personality: Human personality means
nothing to me. Personality isn't what's sacred to me.
If it did, I could easily put out the eyes of anyone as
Oedipus did his own. He still had exactly the same
personality as before. I wouldn't have touched the
person in him, I would only have destroyed his eyes.
What is it? What is it that prevents me from putting
out that man's eyes if I'm allowed to do it and if I
feel like doing it?

CHORUS   Put out his eyes. Burn his thighs. Pull
out his tongue, put it in Washington where it belongs
on the heaps of the other rotting dungs of tongues.

*SIMONE addresses audience, while human pyramids
made by the actors begin slowly to revolve:*

The whole of your being is sacred to me, each one of
you. But you are not sacred in all respects nor from
every point of view. You are not sacred because of your
long bright hair, or your thick wrists, or your strong

long arms, or your kind heart, or the twinkle in your
knowing eye, or even because your thoughts don't
interfere with mine—none of these facts could keep
me from hurting you without the knowledge that if
I were to put out your eyes, your soul would be
lacerated by knowing the pain, and the fact that *harm*
was being done to you.

CHORUS

>AT THE BOTTOM OF YOUR HEART
>FROM THE TIME YOU'RE A BABE
>THOUGH YOU GROW MILES APART
>FROM THE PEOPLE THROUGH WHICH
>YOU WERE MADE

DUET

>YOU EXPECT. YOU EXPECT. YOU EXPECT.

SOPRANO

>WITH THE CERTAINTY AND THE LIGHT
>WHEN THE SPERM ENTERED THE EGG.

BARITONE

>YOU EXPECT TO GO ON BEING REMADE
> AS THE FIRST
>ECSTASY OF THE TRINITY WHEN
> YOU WERE MADE.

*Pyramids disassemble and ENSEMBLE goes into dance
formations.*

CHORUS
YOU WERE MADE
YOU WERE MADE

SOPRANO
YOU WERE MADE IN ECSTASY

BARITONE
LYING DOWN OR STANDING UP,

SOPRANO
CROSSED HORIZONS OR AGAINST THE G.E.

BARITONE
YOU WERE LAID AS YOU WERE MADE.

CHORUS
ECSTASY. ECSTASY. ECSTASY.

SIMONE *(tough and strong)*   There is something in all
of us that goes on indomitably *expecting,* in the teeth of
all experience of crimes committed, suffered, and wit-
nessed, that good.

CHORUS *(softly)*
GOOD. GOOD.

SIMONE   That good and not evil will be done to you.
It is this faith above all that is sacred in every human
being.

ALL   WOO!
Begin to dance.

CHORUS *(like a thirties musical)*
      THIS ABOVE ALL,
      THIS ABOVE ALL,
      THIS ABOVE ALL,
      LEARN TO WALK IN HIGHER HEELS
      THIS ABOVE ALL, BABY
      THIS ABOVE ALL
      LEARN TO WALK LIKE YOU OWN
        THE WORLD

Simone exits.

      LEARN HOW TO KICK AND FLY
      LEARN HOW TO FLY
        WITHOUT GETTING SICK
      LEARN HOW TO THROW AWAY THE STICK
      WHAT YOU DO IS SHOVE IT UP THEIR ASS
      IT'S ESPECIALLY GOOD
        WHEN THEY RUN OUT OF GAS
      AND YOU WANT NERVE
      TO CARRY THE VERVE
      AND SHOW THOSE NIPPLES
      LET THEM RIPPLE
      THIS ABOVE ALL
      GET AS TALL AS YOU CAN BEFORE
      THE GEESE BEGIN
        TO STEP ALL OVER YOU AND

WHEN YOU FALL
WHEN YOU FALL BABY
PRACTICE HOW TO DO IT WITH A SMILE.
I'D WALK A MILLION MILES
FOR ONE OF YOUR LUCKIES
MY BUCKY LITTLE RAG-TIME
   SON-OF-A-BITCH
YOU WITCH
THIS WAS THE DAYS BEFORE GARY
LEARNED TO SWITCH HIS HORSE
AND COCAINE WAS RUNNING A CLOSE
SECOND TO ANYONE'S OPIUM DREAM,
   IT'S A SCREAM
BUT THIS ABOVE ALL,
THIS ABOVE ALL, LEARN HOW
TO LOOK LIKE YOU'RE TALL.
THE FALL IS FUNNIER.
THE FALL IS FUNNIER WHEN YOU FALL
   RIGHT OFF THAT WALL.
OH BE TALL.
THERE MIGHT BE A LIGHT
   OUTSIDE THE GATE,
DON'T YOU SEE IT.
THERE MIGHT BE A LIGHT
   OUTSIDE THE GATE,
DON'T YOU SEE IT.
LET'S BURN GIN TO THAT.
WE NEED A LIGHT TO SHOW
WE'RE RIGHT,
WE'RE RIGHT

        BECAUSE WE KNOW IN THE
        BOTTOMS OF YOUR CUPS
        THAT MIGHT CAN'T CONQUER RIGHT,
        THAT MIGHT CAN'T CONQUER RIGHT, ETC.
        (softer under next two lines)

BARITONE
        THERE IS NO WAR ON.
        THERE IS NO WAR ON.

Blackout.

Series of rapid scenes:

*Out of work MEN of the town are pounding huge stones
with sledge hammers.*

SIMONE   Why are you cracking the rocks?

ONE   We have to.

SIMONE   Are you going to build a wall or a garden.

TWO   We're out of work.

SIMONE   What do you mean you're out of work,
you're working harder than I do.

THREE   We have to do this or they won't give us our unemployment checks.

SIMONE   Give me one of those and I'll help you.

She stands beside the MEN and though she's slower, she still works. Then ALL run to the next scene.

In the factory. The WORKERS are having a sit-in. They sit on the floor, arms linked and swaying, singing the end of "The International." SIMONE is there too, arms linked with the WORKERS, between two men. TWO MEN in charge of running the factory are conferring with one another as the song ends. They turn and shout at the WORKERS.

MANAGER ONE   Seven percent increase.

WORKERS   Fifteen.

MANAGER TWO   Seven percent.

WORKERS   *Fifteen.*

They yell this back and forth in mounting crescendo. Moment of silence.

WORKERS   Fifteen and a joint committee of workers and management.

MANAGER ONE   I'll hire and fire whom I choose.

WORKERS   Joint committee or no work done. Joint committee or no work done.

MANAGER TWO   We'll close down the factory.

MANAGER ONE   We'll close down the factory—that will put some sense into you.

WORKERS   Good, good, good. Close down the factory and we'll take it over and run it ourselves. We run this factory ourselves anyway.

MANAGER ONE   This is a gross infringement of liberty.

WORKERS   We want fifteen percent more.

MANAGER TWO   You make me sick.

WORKERS   Fifteen! Fifteen! Fifteen! Fifteen! Fifteen! We'll make you sick, all right.

Go for the managers' throats—then immediately transform into COMRADES at a meeting.

A political meeting of leftist coalition parties.

SIMONE *(addressing the crowd)*   Friends and fellow workers. Some of us have been greatly troubled and alarmed by news of the continuing purge in Russia. I'm afraid that in this struggle that begins to look like the classic struggle between the conservatives and the innovators the value of life is being forgotten. The conservatives do not know what to conserve, and the innovators do not know what to innovate—

VOICE   Revisionists! Traitorous revisionists!

SIMONE   Please, I ask you to pay one more minute of attention. It's true so far as we know it that Stalin's lieutenant S. M. Kirov was murdered. But Stalin is using this crime as a tool against many comrades who fought and sacrificed many long yea.s to bring Marxist-Leninist concepts into being. If he is allowed to continue unchecked in this "purge," there will be no chance for the dictatorship of the proletariat, because all his brothers will have been eliminated resulting in the dictatorship of one man, Joseph Stalin. We must show him that there is a world of opinion, considered and humane opinion by his brothers in other countries that condemn his actions, that he must cease and desist in this cruel persecution—

ONE   Traitor! She's a Trotskyite.

Some people walk out.

TWO   The purge is just and moral. Those men were

working with the Germans to overthrow Stalin and so
are you. I denounce Simone as a Trotskyite!

THREE   Get her.

FOUR   Beat her up.

They move slowly toward her.

FIVE   Smash her mouth.

SIX   Don't let her open it again.

SEVEN   Kill her.

SIMONE   I'm not a Trotskyite, I belong to no party.
I am against totalitarianism in all its forms. If this
"purge" continues in Russia, Stalin will succeed in
creating a monolithic totalitarian unity and it will be
an end to Lenin's ideals and an end to people's
democracy.

EIGHT   Get her. Trotskyite!

*They grab her. NINE and a small group of friends
holding two guns surround SIMONE to protect her.*

TEN   I support Stalin.

ELEVEN   Shut that Trotskyite's trap.

SIMONE   I'm not a Trotskyite, I'm a Frenchman.

NINE   Simone, comrade, stay in the middle of us. We'll get you out safely.

TWELVE   You're a Trotskyite and you're a Jew!

With some brief scuffling, they get her out of the meeting.

Outside the meeting, SIMONE is talking with MAN who rescued her.

SIMONE   Thank you, Pierre. I'll never forget your kindness and your bravery.

PIERRE   Those Communist fanatics want to drive us into war. You know that during the general strike they were working on the side of management to *prevent our* strike!

SIMONE   I know, because they want all the armaments built as soon as possible to speed up the prospect of war. Well, I'm going off to fight in a war, a just war. I've decided to go to Spain. At least *there*, my one more pair of hands might be useful.

PIERRE   Be careful your rifle doesn't backfire on you, you're not so clever with your hands.

SIMONE   Don't worry. I'm a pacifist. I'll never carry a rifle, there's other work to do.

Blackout.

SIMONE in Spain: on the banks of the Ebro River. The Anarchist forces she has joined are on one side and Fascist forces are on the other. Sound of airplane overhead.

CAPTAIN   Get that plane!

The SQUADRON, including SIMONE, who does have a rifle in hand, begin to shoot. SIMONE lies on her back and shoots straight up into the air.

The pisser's flying too high.

Sound of small bomb exploding.

At least their bombs are getting smaller. That means we're winning.

A small squad of MEN come in dragging TWO PRIESTS.

ONE   Captain! Captain! Look what we found hiding in the rushes on the river bank.

CAPTAIN   This will make forty priests we've shot. *(He points at one of them)*   Kneel with your head in prayer.

The other MEN laugh; SIMONE lowers her rifle. The CAPTAIN shoots the PRIEST. He falls forward and dies, crying out "Jesus" in Spanish.

CAPTAIN *(to the SECOND PRIEST)*   We're going to let you go, so you can tell the rest of your brothers to get the hell out of our country. Get going, on the double.

As the PRIEST turns, he shoots him too. The MEN laugh again. SIMONE throws down her rifle.

Squadron. Attention! We're going out on patrol. The Fascists are just across the river, and at dawn we're going to start picking them off. Simone?

SIMONE   I'll stay in camp and cook.

TWO *(sotto voce, to a comrade)*   Thank God, she's so awkward with a gun, she'll kill one of us one day.

CAPTAIN   Good, you stay and deep-fry me some of those chickens we commandeered. I haven't had fresh meat in two months.

They march off stealthily. SIMONE puts a pot of oil on the fire. Another WOMAN helps her peel vegetables to throw into the oil. They pluck chickens.

SIMONE   Atrocities. On both sides.

WOMAN *(laughing)*   Did you see how the other thought God had saved his life?

SIMONE   How can you laugh at a thing like that?

WOMAN   It was funny. Did you see the look on his face after the bullet hit his head?

SIMONE   This isn't our war. This is nothing but a war fought by Germany against Russia. We're fools and pawns.

She's so angry she hits the pot of oil so hard that it spills over onto her leg. She screams and falls.

WOMAN   Oh, my God, your leg is burning.

She runs out screaming for help.

SIMONE alone in a field hospital reciting math formulas to avoid the pain. Her FATHER and MOTHER rush on.

FATHER   Simone, my precious.

MOTHER   Simone, my own.

FATHER   It's taken us a month to find you.

MOTHER *(not daring to look)*   How bad?

FATHER   What butcher has been tending you? This dressing hasn't been changed in a week, half the flesh is exposed. *(He brings things out of his bag, gives her a sedative.)* Here, this will still the pain.

SIMONE   I'm getting used to it.

MOTHER   We'll take her home to recover.

SIMONE   No, no, father, I have to rejoin my unit.

FATHER   I'm your father and your doctor and you'll do as I say. Let's get a stretcher.

MOTHER and FATHER exit.

SIMONE is alone in her room.
Visitation.

SIMONE   My spirit is sick. Do I have a spirit. Pains
in the throat, double pains. I can't swallow but I feel
constantly that I'll vomit. My spine. My spine is sick.
I can't work and that makes me sicker. Not to be able
to work. No work. Work beating in my head, but my
hands refuse to close around a pencil, my mind won't
work for me, but something in me is working, and I'm
so sick and weak. The struggle against this stupid body
is getting too much to bear. I've got to think my way
out of it but I can't think. My God, my God, I can't
think. I can't move, out of this bed, my God I can't
stand. I can't walk. I can't think, I can't think, this
stupid pain. My God. My God, I need something. I
need something. I need my work. I need to work. Any
work. I'd cry for joy to be able to bend in the dirt and
pick up potatoes till my back ached from work. Honest
work, not the work of fighting this endless headache.
I'll try to vomit. I'll get it out, I'll vomit out the illness.
Oh my God, can't I get any light into my head? My
God! My God! My God!

The ENTIRE CAST comes on stage and lifts SIMONE
up, giving her a total caress. They hum. They take her
pain into their bodies, until all but five who lift her up
to God are feeling the pain that she had.
As they lift SIMONE, they take her clothes off, and as
the clothes fall, other actors put them on, continuing
a pain centered at a point in the body the garment

covers. They left her straight up if they can, her arms
outstretched, smiling with her eyes closed.
They put her down and exit.

LOVE III
The Poem of George Herbert

SIMONE *(transfixed, warmed, and filled with divine*
love, sings)
    LOVE BADE ME WELCOME
        YET MY SOUL DREW BACK,
        GUILTIE OF DUST AND SINNE.
    BUT QUICK-EY'D LOVE,
        OBSERVING ME GROW SLACK
        FROM MY FIRST ENTRANCE IN,
    DREW NEARER TO ME,
        SWEETLY QUESTIONING,
        IF I LACK'D ANY THING.

    A GUEST, I ANSWER'D,
        WORTHY TO BE HERE:
        LOVE SAID, YOU SHALL BE HE.
    I THE UNKINDE, UNGRATEFULL?
        AH MY DEARE,
        I CANNOT LOOK ON THEE.
    LOVE TOOK MY HAND,
        AND SMILING DID REPLY,
        WHO MADE THE EYES BUT I?

TRUTH LORD, BUT I HAVE MARR'D THEM:
   LET MY SHAME GO WHERE
   IT DOTH DESERVE.
AND KNOW YOU NOT, SAYES LOVE,
   WHO BORE THE BLAME?
   MY DEARE, THEN I WILL SERVE.
YOU MUST SIT DOWN, SAYES LOVE,
   AND TASTE MY MEAT:
   SO I DID SIT AND EAT.

ENSEMBLE dancers enter and dance with SIMONE, while the CHORUS sings:

Song for SIMONE, OPERA SINGERS, CHORUS and DANCERS

I BELIEVE GOD CREATED
SO HE COULD BE LOVED
GOD CREATED TO BE LOVED
GOD CREATED AROUND AND ABOVE
SO THAT HE, GOD COULD BE LOVED.

BUT GOD CAN'T CREATE GOD
GOD CAN'T CREATE ANYTHING TO BE GOD

BUT GOD CANNOT BE LOVED BY ANYTHING
WHICH ISN'T GOD, GOD NEEDS
GOD TO SING
GOD NEEDS GOD TO SING TO HIM OF HIS LOVE
   OF GOD FOR GOD
GOD NEEDS GOD TO LOVE HIM INTO GOD.

THIS IS A CONTRADICTION!
NOT A FICTION BUT A PERFECT
A PERFECT, AN EXACT CONTRADICTION.
I HAVE THE CONVICTION
THAT THIS CONTRADICTION
CONTAINS IN ITSELF NECESSITY ITSELF.
THIS IS NOT PERVERSITY
THIS IS NOT MIND PLAY
OR PLAY OF MIND
BUT THIS IS A PERFECT CONTRADICTION
CONTRADICTION CREATES ACTION
THIS IS A CONTRADICTION THAT DEFINES
NECESSITY. NECESSITY. *NECESSITY!*

BUT EVERY CONTRADICTION
HAS THE CONDITION OF RESOLVING
ITSELF THROUGH THE PROCESS
THROUGH THE PROCESS
THROUGH THE PROCESS OF
BECOMING, BECOMING, BECOMING
BECOMING *BECOMING!*

GOD CREATED ME TO SEE THE SEA
AND TO LOVE HIM
AND TO LOVE HIM
"I"—"I"—"I" THIS FINITE BEING
I THIS THIS "I"
"I" AND "I," THIS LITTLE "I"
I CAN'T LOVE GOD
UNTIL

UNTIL, THROUGH THE ACTION OF GRACE
THAT TAKES OVER THE EMPTY SPACE
OF MY TOTAL SOUL—
THE GRACE THAT FILLS MY SOUL
THE GRACE TO MAKE ME WHOLE WITH GOD.

AND AS THE LITTLE "I" DISAPPEARS
GOD LOVES HIMSELF
GOD LOVES HIMSELF

BY MY GIVING UP MY "I"
AS I BECOME NOT "I"
AS I CANNOT SEE THE SKY, NOR BE THE SKY
GOD LOVES ME AS I DISAPPEAR

I GIVE GOD TO GOD AND
AND GOD LOVES HIMSELF
AS THIS PROCESS GOES ON FOREVER
THEREFORE GOD
HAS CREATED TIME
TIME IS INDIFFERENT TO ME,
THERE IS ALL THE TIME
IN MY SHORT WORLD
FOR ME TO BECOME NOT ME

SO THAT GOD
SO THAT GOD CAN LOVE HIMSELF
THIS
THIS
THIS

THIS
THIS
THIS IS THE NECESSITY, THE NECESSITY,
THE NECESSITY.

NECESSITY!

A police station, three POLICEMEN and a SECRETARY.

ONE   It's been reported that you are a Gaulliste.

TWO   You were seen distributing *Témoignage chrétien.*

THREE   An illegal paper.

SIMONE   It has a higher literary style than the government censors.

TWO   So you admit to this underground activity.

SIMONE   I admit that I read everything I can get my hands on.

ONE   If you don't tell us who the rest of your comrades are. . .

TWO   You'll go to prison.

THREE   And I'll personally see that you, a teacher of philosophy, will be put into the same cells as the prostitutes.

ONE   As the prostitutes.

SIMONE   Why I've always wanted to know about such circles of women. It will be a very good opportunity to get to know them. Yes, please do send me to jail.

TWO   She's crazy.

THREE   She's crazy, no professor of philosphy would want to associate with filthy prostitutes.

SIMONE   But I would. It's a subject I haven't had time to study yet.

ONE   Release the prisoner. She's crazy.

Blackout.

SIMONE arrives in Marseilles and goes to the Dominican monastery where she can ask a PRIEST who is helping people to get out of the country for work while she waits to get out too. There are several PEOPLE before her, one is in his office and is just leaving.

MAN   Thank you for getting me the passport, Father, it's saved my life.

FATHER *(a warm man with natural charm)*
Safe journey and God bless, my son.

SIMONE *(enters shyly)*   Excuse me, Father. I hate to take away from your valuable time, but I need some sort of work, preferably manual labor, where I can fade into a group. Is there any farm work about, perhaps the grape harvest?

FATHER   My child, you look so frail, I hardly. . .

SIMONE   I'm not as frail as I look—I've worked in factories.

FATHER   You don't speak like a factory worker.

SIMONE   You know about the laws: we're not allowed to work. My family and I are bound for Morocco on our way to the States. I want to work to occupy my time.

FATHER   Are you sure you can manage. The sun's hot.

SIMONE   Good.

FATHER   I have a friend, just outside of town who
might take you on...

SIMONE   Thank you Father... Father... may I come
to speak with you sometime again...

FATHER   I'm taken up with many duties besides my
clerical ones—so many people are being hounded down
by the police, so many people need help and advice.

SIMONE   I'd like to speak to you about Christ.

*They freeze, walk in a circle. She hesitantly approaches
him again.*

SIMONE   After working in the factories, I finally
understood affliction. I began to see myself as a slave
and I was often able to rise above the physical affliction
of my headaches. Then in a Chapel in Solesmes where
I'd gone to hear the Gregorian music at Easter I was
able to listen to the music in spite of pain. By an extreme effort of attention I was able to get outside this
miserable flesh, leaving it to suffer by itself, and I found
a pure and perfect joy in the unspeakable beauty of the
chanting and the words. During the time I was there I
also met a young man, a messenger I think of him now,
who introduced me to George Herbert's poem "Love."
From then on whenever my headache would reach a

painful crisis, I would recite this poem fixing all my attention on it, clinging with all my soul to the tenderness it enshrines. One day, while saying this poem with all my attention, Christ Himself came down and He took possession of me.

FATHER   Did you see Him?

SIMONE   No, it was the presence of love, of infinite love, a certainty of love, a love which I have never sought and which I'd never thought existed.

FATHER   My child, are you seeking Catholic instruction?

SIMONE   I don't wish Baptism.

FATHER   But that is complete union..

SIMONE   I prefer to stand at the door of the church.

FATHER   Then you're still a long way from Christianity.

Again they freeze, walk in a small circle, relax, and she approaches him again.

SIMONE   Every day before I go out to harvest I say the "Our Father" in Greek. I try to do this with the utmost attention and if I do, Christ comes nearer to me now than He did that first time.

FATHER   It gives me joy to see the light growing within you.

They freeze, she kneels and says the Pater Noster in Greek, or any language the actress would like. Then she stands. They approach each other again.

FATHER   My child, you suffer too much from your former intellectual life. You're confusing reality with distortions of it. I feel you're hardest and most severe in your judgments on that which could touch you the most.

SIMONE   I have to beware of you. Friendship and the power of suggestion is what I'm most susceptible to.

FATHER   But Baptism is—

SIMONE   I don't want to belong to any groups. I want to be invisible, so that I can move among all groups. I'm suspicious of structures, and especially the structure of the Catholic Church, it has been totalitarian since the time of the Roman Empire.

FATHER   You're still locked into the narrow philosophy of Spinoza.

SIMONE   I'd never read any of the mystics till my love of Christ, but now I see that Dionysus and Osiris are an early form of Christ. The *Bhagavad-Gita* when read aloud is a marvelous Christian sound. Yes, even

113

Plato was a mystic. I see the *Iliad* now as bathed in Christian light.

FATHER   Your early intellectual training and culture are keeping you from contemplating the true mysteries of the Church dogma. Baptism is a complete union.

SIMONE   I want to thank you for bearing with me for so long. I'd never really considered the problem of Baptism as a practical one before. I'm sorry to withhold from you what would give you the greatest joy, but God has other uses for me. If I felt His command to be baptized, I would come running at once. For now I think God doesn't want me in the Church, perhaps at the moment of death. . .

FATHER   It's my only concern that you stay in readiness. . .

SIMONE   I could only say all this to you because I'm leaving tomorrow. Goodbye, you've been a father and a brother to me. . . It's impossible to think of you without thinking of God.

Exit.

Outside a Harlem church. Sounds of Gospel music.

CLAIRE   We're the only white people here. Are you sure we won't offend?

SIMONE   I've been to a different church in Harlem every Sunday since I arrived in New York.

CLAIRE   I'm a bit uneasy.

SIMONE   Are you my friend?

CLAIRE   Yes, you know it; we've talked for days and nights together.

SIMONE   Will you be my friend?

CLAIRE   We're going to get back to France together; we're going to sabotage the Nazis together.

SIMONE   Come, let's enter this church of God.

CLAIRE presses Simone's hand and they enter the church together. A song is ending and they sit in first row of auditorium.

PREACHER   Brothers and Sisters, let us pray for our President. Let us pray for our great President Franklin Delano Roosevelt. He faces trying times in this terrible war. The people on the East is attacking us, and the people in the West is attacking us. Brothers and Sisters,

let us pray to Jesus to help our President in these terrible
times so that with the help of You, oh Lord, and Your
chosen Son, Jesus, our President Roosevelt can make
peace all over God's great, green and beautiful garden.

Give yourself up to the power of Our Lord,
Give yourself up to the power of Our Lord,
If you ever gonna find yourself
You got to give yourself up,
Give yourself up to the power of Our Lord.

PREACHER *(sings)*
    BROTHERS AND SISTERS
    BROTHERS AND SISTERS
    WHAT SEX IS JESUS?
    WHAT SEX IS GOD?

CHORUS *(repeats and claps)*
    WHAT SEX IS JESUS?
    WHAT SEX IS GOD?

PREACHER
    WHAT SEX WAS MARY?
    WHAT SEX WAS SAUL
      AFTER HE CHANGED HIS NAME TO PAUL?
    JESUS LETS US INTO HIM
    BOTH MEN AND WOMEN
    JESUS LETS US INTO HIM
    BOTH SAINTS AND SINNIN'

MALE SINGER   Simone, Simone, Simone. Your

body is women and your head talks to God. *(Brings SIMONE on stage.)*

CHORUS
> JESUS HAD A PRICK
> HE DIDN'T USE TO FUCK WITH
> BUT PENETRATING THE WATERS
> HE MADE ENOUGH FISHES TO
>   FEED THE MULTITUDE
> WITHOUT LICKING ESSENTIAL OILS, JESUS
> MADE BREAD WITHOUT AN OVEN
> HE FED A THOUSAND DOZENS

CLAIRE   Simone, I feel I have to leave. I'm overcome with emotion, I feel I might dissolve. Let's go before I can't control myself any longer.

SIMONE   Get up with the congregation. Let's go with them to Jesus.

CLAIRE   I'm afraid.

SIMONE   You're ready to face the Nazis, but you're still not ready to approach God?

They rise and join the congregation, who are singing and jitterbugging and throwing themselves into a trance with their closeness to the Lord.

A woman leaps up from the congregation. She is possessed and sings. The CHORUS echoes her.

WOMAN

>OH LORD, OH LORD, OH LORD
>I'M OPENING UP FOR YOU
>OH LORD, OH LORD,
>>I'M READY TO RECEIVE
>MY JESUS,
>OH JESUS, SON OF GOD,
>>I'LL DO YOU RIGHT
>OH JESUS, SON OF GOD,
>>I'LL DO RIGHT TO YOU

>MY ARMS ARE OPEN
>MY ARMS ARE OPEN
>OH LORD, OH JESUS,
>>I'LL GIVE IT ALL BACK TO YOU.
>TAKE MY HANDS
>TAKE MY FEET

(Repeat all the parts of the body till end of scene.)

CHORUS

>SHE'S A JESUS LADY
>SHE'S A JESUS LADY
>WHAT SEX IS JESUS?
>JESUS DONE ENTERED HER
>JESUS DONE ENTERED HER
>JESUS DONE ENTERED HER

PREACHER

>SHE'S A JESUS LADY
>SHE'S A JESUS LADY

SHE'S A JESUS LADY
RIGHT NOW AND FOREVERMORE.

Exit.

French headquarters in England
As this scene progresses it should be as if SIMONE is
visiting a series of offices. Each official, and, if possible,
his secretary too, gets taller and fatter, until the final
one is a giant figure somewhat like De Gaulle.
On screens and slides, on scrolls, that come down, from
projections, etc., we should see films and stills of people
in their death agonies.

SIMONE   *Bonjour, mon cher ami.* It's good to see
you again. I had no idea how long it would take me to
get to London.

MAN   Did you go to America?

SIMONE   Only because I thought it would be a faster
way to get here, so that I can be of service to France. It
took much longer than I'd hoped.

MAN   Your parents?

SIMONE   They wanted to escape from the anti-
Semitism without being separated from me. I've come
to offer you my services to work for France. I distribu-

ted one of the most important clandestine publications in the free zone, *Les Cahiers du témoignage chrétien.* But when I was there, I was consoled by sharing the suffering of my country. I've come back to offer myself, because France's misfortunes hurt me much more at a distance than when I was there. Leaving was like tearing up my roots. But I only left in the hope that I could take a bigger and more effective part in the efforts, dangers and sufferings of this great struggle. I have an idea.

MAN   Perhaps you'd like to explain it to the Captain?

CAPTAIN *(enters and bows)*   *Mademoiselle.*

SIMONE   I have an idea.

CAPTAIN   *Bon*, they are needed.

SIMONE   This idea will save the lives of many soldiers.

CAPTAIN   *Bon.*

SIMONE   Many needless deaths happen on the battle-field due to the lack of immediate care, cases of shock, exposure, loss of blood.

CAPTAIN   Correct.

SIMONE   Please consider it seriously, I want to work
in secret operations, preferably dangerous.

CAPTAIN   Perhaps you should speak to the major.
(Exits.)

MAJOR *(enters)*   *Mademoiselle.*

SIMONE   I really believe I can be useful. I appeal to
you as a comrade to get me out of this painful moral
situation. A lot of people don't understand why it's
a painful moral situation, but you certainly do. We had
a great deal in common when we were students together.
It gave me a real joy to learn that you have such an important position in London. I'm relying on you.

MAJOR   We can certainly use your brilliant mind.
You were first in your class.

SIMONE   I want action. Here's the idea: create a
special body of front-line nurses.

MAJOR   Of women?

SIMONE *(nods and hurries on)*   It would be a very
mobile organization and should always be at the points
of greatest danger.

MAJOR   But the horrors of war at the front—

SIMONE   —are so distinct today in everyone's imagination that one can regard any woman who is capable of volunteering for such work as being very probably capable of performing it.

MAJOR   But they risk certain death.

SIMONE   They would need to have a good deal of courage. They would need to offer their lives as a sacrifice.

MAJOR   But we have never put our women in such danger. That's why we men leave for the front to defend our homes and families.

SIMONE   There is no reason to regard the life of a woman, especially if she has passed her first youth without marrying or having children, as more valuable than a man's life. All the less so if she has accepted the risk of death.

MAJOR   But how to regulate . . .

SIMONE   Simply make mothers, wives and girls below a certain age ineligible.

MAJOR   I'm considering the idea.

SIMONE   The moral support would be inestimable. They would comfort the men's last moments, they would mitigate by their presence and their words the agony of waiting for the arrival of the stretcher-bearers. You must understand the essential role played in the present war by moral factors. They count for very much more than in past wars. It's one of the main reasons for Hitler's successes that he was the first to see this.

MAJOR   I believe you should explain this to the General. *(Exits.)*

General enters, only nods.

SIMONE *(exhorting)*   Hitler has never lost sight of the essential need to strike everybody's imagination; his own people's, his enemies', and the innumerable spectators'. One of his most effective instruments has been the SS. These men are unmoved by suffering and death, either for themselves or for all the rest of humanity. Their heroism originates from an extreme brutality that corresponds perfectly to the spirit of the regime and the designs of their leader. We cannot copy these methods of Hitler's. First, because we fight in a different spirit and with different motives. But when it is a question of striking the imagination, copies never succeed. Only the new is striking. We give a lot of thought to propaganda for the rear, yet it is just as important at the front. At the rear, propaganda is carried on by words. At the front, verbal propaganda must be replaced by the propaganda of action.

GENERAL   What do you propose?

SIMONE   A simple corps of women performing a few
humane services in the very center of the battle—the
climax of inhumanity—would be a signal defiance of the
inhumanity which the enemy has chosen for himself and
which he also compels us to practice. A small group of
women exerting day after day a courage of this kind
with a maternal solicitude would be a spectacle so new,
so much more striking than Hitler's young SS fanatics.
The contrast between these women and the SS would
make a more telling argument than any propaganda
slogan. It would illustrate with supreme clarity the
two roads between which humanity today is forced
to choose.

GENERAL   *Merci.* A very good idea. We will think
about it. In the meantime we have some essential work
for you to do.

Typewriter and mounds of papers are wheeled out.

Four copies of each as soon as possible. There's a
war on.

*Blackout. The OLD MEN pull the cord attached to their
cherub and ashes, bones and plastic baby dolls shower
the audience.*

SIMONE, with a mike on a high platform, addresses a crowd. As she speaks, lights begin to go off and on. Strange noises—gunshot. Bit by bit the PEOPLE leave and take up sides to fight the war.

SIMONE   We're in a conflict with no definable objective. When there is no objective, there is no common measure of proportion. Compromise is inconceivable. The only way the importance of such a battle can be measured is by the sacrifices it demands. From this it follows that the sacrifices already made are a perpetual argument for new sacrifices. There would never be any reason to stop killing and dying, except that there is fortunately a limit to human endurance.

Silence.

This paradox is so extreme as to defy analysis. And yet the most perfect example of it is known to every so-called educated man, but, by a sort of taboo, we read it without understanding. The Greeks and Trojans massacred one another for ten years on account of Helen. Not one of them except the dilettante warrior Paris cared two straws about her. All of them wished she'd never been born. Its importance was simply imagined as corresponding to the deaths incurred and the further massacres expected.

Lights flicker and go out. PEOPLE crawl in aisles and over audience. Lights—flashing; crying, running.

This implied an importance beyond all reckoning. Hector foresaw that his city would be destroyed, his father and brothers massacred, his wife degraded to a slavery worse than death. Achilles knew that he was condemning his father to the miseries and humiliations of a defenseless old age. All of them were aware that their long absence at the war would bring ruin on their homes; yet no one felt the cost too great, because they were all in pursuit of a literal non-entity whose only value was in the *price paid for it!*

Silence—then the war begins again.

For the clear-sighted, there is no more distressing symptom of this truth than the unreal character of most of the conflicts that are taking place today. They have even less reality than the war between Greeks and Trojans. At the heart of the Trojan War there was at least a woman, and what is more, a woman of perfect beauty. For our contemporaries the role of Helen is played by words with capital letters. If we grasp one of these words, all swollen with blood and tears, and squeeze it, we find it is empty.

Silence—then just breathing. Then war begins again.

Words with content and meaning are not murderous. When empty words are given capital letters, then men on the slightest pretext will begin shedding blood. In these conditions the only definition of success is to crush a rival group of men who have a hostile word on their banners. When a word is properly defined, it loses its capital letter and can no longer serve either as a banner or as a hostile slogan.

Screams. Someone is shot while pleading not to be. Silence.

It becomes simply a sign, helping us to grasp some concrete reality, concrete objective or method of activity. To clarify thought, to discredit the intrinsically meaningless words and to define the use of others by precise analysis—to do this, strange though it may appear, might be a way of saving human lives.

BARITONE   How like a woman to reduce war to semantics.

SOPRANO   How like a man to reduce war to mathematics.

All the MEN are lying on stage or in aisles. The WOMEN drag their bodies to a pile on stage as SIMONE speaks.

SIMONE   My dearest brothers, lying twenty years in your hospital beds, you are privileged men. The present state of the world is reality for you. You are experiencing more reality in your constant affliction than those who are dying in the war, at this moment killing and dying, wounded and being wounded. Because they are taken unaware. They don't know where they are. They don't know what is happening to them. People not in the middle of the war don't know what's real. But you men have been repeating in thought, for twenty years, that act which took and then released so many men. But you were seized permanently. And now the war is here again to kill millions of men. You are ready to think. Or if you are still not quite ready—as I feel you are not—you only have the thinnest shell to break before emerging from the darkness inside the egg into the light of truth. It is a very ancient image. The egg is this world we see. The bird in it is Love, the Love which is God Himself and which lives in the depths of every man, though at first as an invisible seed.

MAN   Will you help me kill myself.

SIMONE   Break your shell and you will no longer be inside. Space is opened and torn apart.

Silence for a moment. In pain and twitching like the men, Simone's voice at first mirrors migraine pain, but then rises above the pain through the speech.

The spirit throws the miserable body in some corner and is transported to a point outside space. Space has become an infinity. The moment stands still.

WOMEN *(singing, facing audience from stage or in position in aisles)*
        THE MOMENT STANDS STILL!

sing

THE MOMENT STANDS STILL!
THE MOMENT STANDS STILL!
THE MOMENT STANDS STILL!
THE MOMENT STANDS STILL!
THE SILENCE IS DENSE
SOUNDS
SOUNDS
SILENCE IS
THE WHOLE OF SPACE IS FILLED
NOT AN ABSENCE OF SOUND
BUT THE MOMENT IS FILLED
WITH THE SECRET WORD
ONCE YOU BREAK OUT OF YOUR SHELL
YOU WILL KNOW WHAT IS REAL
ABOUT WAR
YOU WILL KNOW THE SECRET WORD
YOU NEVER KNEW BEFORE
NOT THE ABSENCE OF SOUND
BUT LOVE, LOVE, LOVE, LOVE, LOVE.

SIMONE *(speaking)*   It is not an absence of sound, but
a positive object of sensation.
Singing:
YOU, WHEN YOU'VE EMERGED
FROM THE SHELL,
WILL KNOW THE REALITY OF WAR.
THE MOST PRECIOUS REALITY TO KNOW
IS THAT, WAR IS UNREALITY ITSELF.
Speaking: You are infinitely privileged. War has
permanently lodged in your body.

WOMEN *(singing)*
[handwritten: 5 in at anna]
    WAR IS AFFLICTION,
    FORTUNATE ARE YOU TO KNOW.

SIMONE   War is affliction. It isn't easy to direct one's thoughts toward affliction voluntarily. To think affliction, it's necessary to bear it in one's flesh, driven very far in like a nail, and for a long time, so that thought may have time to grow strong enough to regard it.

WOMEN *(singing)*
[handwritten: 5 in a alternate]
    WAR IS AFFLICTION,
      FORTUNATE ARE WE TO KNOW.
    FORTUNATE ARE WE.
    WAR IS AFFLICTION.
    FORTUNATELY WE CANNOT SEE IT.
[handwritten: together]   WAR IS AFFLICTION.

SIMONE   You have the opportunity and the function of knowing the truth of the world's affliction. Contemplate its reality!

MEN rise and take their places facing the audience. SIMONE begins to move through them, climbing ever higher on the platforms.

MAN ONE   Eat, Simone. *[handwritten: 5 in d]*

She shakes her head and moves up ramp.

MAN TWO   Eat, Simone.   *anna*

*She shakes head and climbs to highest platform. She's
weak and must hold onto the bars to stand up.
An ACTRESS mounts an auditorium platform and
mechanically intones.*

Tina
WOMAN DOCTOR *(at an inquest, British accent)*
I tried to persuade Simone to take some food, and she   *anna*
said she would try. She did not eat, however, and gave   *p + Penny*
as a reason the thought of her people in France <u>starving</u>.

ENSEMBLE whispers: "Strange suicide" over and over.

She died on the twenty-fourth of August, and death was
due to cardiac failure due to degeneration through
starvation.

anna
BARITONE *(singing, as a judge)*   Simone, aged thirty-
four, committed suicide by starvation while the balance
of her mind was disturbed.

CHORUS speaks:

WOMEN   Strange suicide. Strange suicide.

MEN   Refused to eat. – *Tina*

WOMEN   Strange suicide. Strange suicide.

131

MEN   Refused to eat. *Sina*

MEN AND WOMEN *(as lights begin to dim on
ENSEMBLE)*   She refused. She refused. She refused. *all*

WOMAN ONE *anna*   She wouldn't eat. She wouldn't eat
the bombs of the Germans, she wouldn't eat the furnaces
of the Nazis. She swallowed the pride of France, but it
didn't stick to her ribs.

CHORUS   Strange, strange, strange, strange, strange— *all*
Simone wouldn't eat.
Simone wouldn't eat.

WOMAN TWO *Sina*   Her soul was full, she didn't have to
eat. There's no such thing as a personality. There's no
such thing as a mind when the body dies. The mind can
die before the body dies. *Penny*

WOMAN THREE   She wouldn't eat. She wouldn't eat.
She couldn't eat when others starved. She wouldn't eat
while Hitler carved the meat of her countryside.

WOMAN FOUR *anna*   While everyone else lived on spoiled
cabbage leaves and boiled rainwater, Simone ate nothing.

Blackout on ENSEMBLE. *Sina*

WOMAN FIVE   How thin she must have been. What
a tiny coffin they must have buried her in.

132

Pin spot on SIMONE, dimming slowly, slowly, slowly, slowly to black.

Plays by Megan Terry
(listed in the order in which they were written)

Ex-Miss Copper Queen on a Set of Pills
> *The People vs. Ranchman and Ex-Miss Copper Queen on a Set of Pills: Two Plays.* New York: Samuel French, Inc., 1968.
>
> *Playwrights for Tomorrow.* Vol. 1, ed. Arthur H. Ballet. Minneapolis: University of Minnesota Press, 1966.

The Magic Realists
> *Best Short Plays of 1968*, ed. Stanley Richards. New York: Chilton Book Co., 1968.
>
> *The Magic Realists, Sanibel and Captiva, One More Little Drinkie.* New York: Samuel French, Inc., 1971.

**The People vs. Ranchman*
> *The People vs. Ranchman and Ex-Miss Copper Queen on a Set of Pills: Two Plays.* New York: Samuel French, Inc., 1968.

**Calm Down Mother

> *Calm Down Mother*. New York: Samuel French, Inc., 1966
>
> *Eight Plays from Off-Off Broadway*, eds. Nick Orzel and Michael Smith. New York: Bobbs-Merrill Co., Inc., 1966.

*Keep Tightly Closed in a Cool Dry Place

> *TDR*, X:4 (Summer, 1966).
>
> *Viet Rock and Other Plays*. New York: Simon and Schuster, 1966.

*Comings and Goings

> *Viet Rock and Other Plays*. New York: Simon and Schuster, 1967.

The Gloaming, Oh My Darling

> *Viet Rock and Other Plays*. New York: Simon and Schuster, 1967.

*Viet Rock

> *TDR*, XI:1 (Fall, 1966).
>
> *Viet Rock and Other Plays*. New York: Simon and Schuster, 1967.

Home

> *Megan Terry's Home, or Future Soap*. New York: Samuel French, Inc., 1973

Sanibel and Captiva

> *The Magic Realists, Sanibel and Captiva, One More*

Little Drinkie. New York: Samuel French, Inc.,
1971.

Massachusetts Trust
  Spontaneous Combustion Plays, ed. Rochelle
  Owens. New York: Winter House, 1972.

The Tommy Allen Show
  Scripts, I:2 (December, 1971)

One More Little Drinkie
  *The Magic Realists, Sanibel and Captiva, One More
  Little Drinkie*. New York: Samuel French, Inc.,
  1971.

*These plays have been translated into every major language in
the world.

**These plays have been translated into French, German,
Dutch, and all Scandanavian languages.

Bibliography of Works By and About
Simone Weil Available in English

By Simone Weil

—— *First and Last Notebooks* (2 vols.), trans. Richard
Rees. London: Oxford University Press, 1970.

—— *The Iliad or, The Poem of Force*, trans. Mary
McCarthy, Pendle Hill, Pennsylvania: A Pendle
Hill Pamphlet, 1945.

—— *Intimations of Christianity*, ed. and trans.
Elisabeth Chase Geissbuhler. London: Routledge
and Kegan Paul, 1957.

—— *Letter to a Priest*, trans. Arthur Wills. London:
Routledge and Kegan Paul, 1953; New York: G.P.
Putnam's Sons, 1954.

—— *The Need for Roots: Prelude to a Declaration of
Duties Toward Mankind*, trans. Arthur Wills.
Preface by T.S. Eliot. New York: G.P. Putnam's
Sons, 1952; New York: Harper Torchbooks, 1971.

—— *Notebooks* (2 vols.), trans. Arthur Wills. New
York: G.P. Putnam's Sons, 1956.

—— *On Science and Necessity and the Love of God*,
trans. Richard Rees. London: Oxford University
Press, 1968.

—— *Oppression and Liberty*, trans. Arthur Wills and John Petrie. London: Routledge and Kegan Paul, 1958.

—— *Selected Essays, 1934-1943*, trans. Richard Rees. London: Oxford University Press, 1962.

—— *Seventy Letters*, trans. Richard Rees. London: Oxford University Press, 1965.

—— *Waiting on God*, trans. Emma Craufurd. London: Routledge and Kegan Paul, 1951; New York: G.P. Putnam's Sons, 1951 (as *Waiting for God*).

About Simone Weil

Cabaud, Jacques. *Simone Weil: A Fellowship in Love.* New York: Channel Press, 1964.

Davy, Marie-Magdeleine. *The Mysticism of Simone Weil*, trans. Cynthia Rowland. London: Rockliff Publishing Corporation, 1951; Boston: Beacon Press, 1951.

Perrin, J.M., and Thibon, G. *Simone Weil As We Knew Her*, trans. Emma Craufurd. London: Routledge and Kegan Paul, 1953.

Rees, Richard. *Simone Weil, A Sketch for a Portrait*, Carbondale, Illinois: Southern Illinois University Press, 1966.

Rees, Richard. *Brave Men: A Study of D.H. Lawrence and Simone Weil*. London: Victor Gollancz, 1958; Carbondale, Illinois: Southern Illinois University Press, 1959.

Tomlin, E.W.F. *Simone Weil*. New Haven: Yale University Press, 1954.

For an extensive list of articles, essays, letters, poems, and other books in French, see the bibliography in the Jacques Cabaud volume on Simone Weil.

Phyllis Jane Wagner received her Ph.D. in theatre from the University of Denver where she was instrumental in creating The Second Season, a producing unit for avant-garde plays. She has directed many; her dissertation was on Megan Terry. She is now director of Liberi Artisti, a traveling repertory troupe.

The Feminist Press is a non-profit, tax-exempt educational and publishing group organized to challenge sexual stereotypes in books and schools and libraries.

We are engaged in a number of educational projects designed to re-examine the ways in which children learn sex roles: members of The Press are advising school systems about their textbooks and providing in-service courses for teachers. We also offer, to students and teachers, free copies of our bibliographies of literature on sex-stereotyping in schools and in children's books, and Feminist Press teacher's guides to the use of our books on the lives of women.

Our publications program includes a series of feminist biographies of women and a series of reprints of important though neglected feminist works from the past, as well as a series of nonsexist children's books. In our adult books, we are interested in helping to recreate the history of women, in discovering how women have been educated and what they have achieved.

A complete listing of our publications appears in our poster-catalogue, available on request.

FEMINIST PRESS BIOGRAPHIES ($1.50)
Elizabeth Barrett Browning by Mary Jane Lupton
Elizabeth Cady Stanton by Mary Ann B. Oakley
Constance de Markievicz by Jacqueline Van Voris

FEMINIST PRESS REPRINTS
The Yellow Wallpaper by Charlotte Perkins Gilman. With an afterword by Elaine R. Hedges ($1.25)
Life in the Iron Mills by Rebecca Harding Davis. With a biographical interpretation by Tillie Olsen ($1.95)
Daughter of Earth by Agnes Smedley ($2.50)

FEMINIST PRESS BOOKS FOR CHILDREN
The Dragon and the Doctor by Barbara Danish ($1.00)
Challenge to Become a Doctor: The Story of Elizabeth Blackwell by Leah Heyn, with illustrations by Greta Handschuh ($1.50)
Firegirl by Gibson Rich, with illustrations by Charlotte Purrington Farley ($1.95)
Nothing but a Dog by Bobbi Katz, with illustrations by Esther Gilman ($1.50)

A. O. Smith can do what she does
because of J. Chaiken +
open theatre →
   Chaiken - (Terry, et al)
   Big Daddy
   M. Terry - On M. T., App. Simon